NEW DIRECTIONS IN ECONOMIC POLICY

NEW DIRECTIONS IN ECONOMIC POLICY

M. L. Burstein

Ye cannot serve God and Mammon
St Matthew, vi, 24

First published 1978 by
THE MACMILLAN PRESS LTD
London and Basingstoke
Associated companies in Delhi,
Dublin, Hong Kong, Johannesburg, Lagos,
Melbourne, New York, Singapore, Tokyo

British Library Cataloguing in Publication Data

Burstein, Meyer
    New directions in economic policy
    1. Economics
    I. Title
    330   HB171

ISBN 978-1-349-03618-9   ISBN 978-1-349-03616-5 (eBook)
                              DOI 10.1007/978-1-349-03616-5

Text set in 10/11 pt Photon Baskerville

This book is for Mavis Cole

Si l'idée de la mort, dans ce temps-là, m'avait, on l'a vu, assombri l'amour, depuis longtemps déjà le souvenir de l'amour m'aidait à ne pas craindre la mort.
Marcel Proust, *À la recherche du temps perdu:* xv, *Le temps retrouvé*, p. 217.

Contents

Preface

This book reflects a wide range of experience in a number of places. It has had a long gestation, but was written fairly quickly in order to remain topical. It quite obviously is an American's book, but part of it was written in England; I hope it is sensitive to British nuances.

The book was written very much alone. During the writing sessions, I came to realize more than ever how good were my teachers in the College of the University of Chicago and how much I owe to my late sister.

I wish economics were easier. Still, if economics were much easier, there would be less need for the book.

New York, August 1977   MB

1 Introduction

1.1 Preliminary Remarks

In my time there have been two cardinal shifts in the direction of economic policy.

Inflation, rather than unemployment, commands the centre of attention now. Furthermore, unemployment is seen as more of a structural than a 'keynesian' problem and the trade-offs between inflation and unemployment are perceived differently.

State intervention in economic affairs has greatly increased, especially in the United States; Franklin Roosevelt initiated processes in America that were well advanced in Europe long before 1933.

The *étatisque* movement masks a sharp directional change in political economy. As late as 1945, reform in the West had class overtones of a vaguely marxian sort: men of the Left or the Left-Centre wanted 'workers' to have fairer shares, greater security, etc. The protagonists in the political–economic struggle had recognizably marxian shapes. Not now. The set of issues contained in '(Ralph) naderism' reflects a sort of *trahison des clercs*. 'Consumerism' is alien to the marxist catechism and adverse to the development policies of the Socialist-bloc regimes, typically insensitive to environmental consequences of their plans for conventional economic growth; consumerism is the child of the rich, not the poor. Nor are the poor emotionally committed to the inner cities they hope to leave; the 'inner city' is a bourgeois concern. Most conservation issues find workers allied with entrepreneurs against a new sort of bourgeois-based Left; materialism, natural to the poor and bound up in their hopes for an easier life, has become a *bête noire* to many heirs to business fortunes.

The French scene in Summer 1977 throws all of this into sharp relief. France is being torn to pieces by forces engendered by its earlier 'economic miracle'; its traditionally humanistically educated intellectuals, enraged by their insignificance in a rapidly industrializing society, have allied themselves in a *union de gauche* with the recently stalinist French Communist Party.

The vast expansion of the public sectors of such countries as the

United States has been one of a number of sources of thrust to expansion of a bureaucratic *Weltanschauung* on the commanding heights of Western societies: the business sector operates with vast armies of *fonctionnaires* more like civil servants than the entrepreneurs described by Adam Smith or Alfred Marshall; lawyers, doctors, engineers, computer experts *et al.*, the components of the huge technocratic and professional forces operating in parallel with business managements, have guild psychologies. American and other entrepreneurial classes are increasingly isolated. The British instance is especially pronounced: talented young people are eager to be posted to 'Versailles' (the eternal symbol of a bloated state-establishment); they aspire to become ranking mandarins planning for, regulating, coordinating, making 'socially responsible' the productive sector of the economy. A different sort of Church has come to occupy the space long vacated by the Church of Christendom.

The increased political·economic weight of the state, *cum* the burgeoning of industrial bureaucraticism, has transformed—Liberals would say reformed—the processes controlling policy formation in the West. Not only are there relatively so many more non-productive members of the economy, their influence now is also politically predominant; in the salons of Georgetown or the charming London townhouses described by Iris Murdoch, the 'quality of life' (whose life?) matters more than macro-economic expansion. Nor do the combination rooms of the ancient colleges much favour materialistic development. The inevitable consequences of the new consensus amongst the new elites are economic stagnation, rising unemployment in a labour force now bounded away from performing 'demeaning' work and an overall sense of enervation easily giving way to boredom. The new political·economic balance of power is strangling private capitalism; the screw turns ever tighter, producing consequences fulfilling the gloomy prophecies of those who demand state intervention in order to 'correct' the faults of capitalism; a destructive process is under way, one that appears cumulative, in the manner of the nuclear processes the new elites abhor in their industrial applications.

1.2 New Perceptions of Economic Events

This book is meant to deepen the reader's understanding of such problems as inflation, unemployment, economic growth, conservation, competition for resources between public and private sectors, etc. as they have developed in a radically-changed socio-political–economic ambience. The more or less objective aspects of economic policy are analysed in Chapters 2–7. Chapters 8 and 9, *Fairness* and *Efficiency*, comprising Part III, *Economics and Ethics*, deal with some philosophical and ethical underpinnings of economic policy; the *truths*, if any, in Part III are of a different order than those of Chapters 2–7; the propositions of Chapters 2–7 can become *known* whilst those of Chapters 8 and 9 can at best only be *revealed*.

Turning to the more or less objective matter of Chapters 2–7, we shall find that economic policy has turned towards new directions not only because of the fundamental ideological transformations already limned but also because of objective shifts in observation, integration and inter-pretation. Naturally, in a science it is impossible to disentangle altogether changes in perceived characteristics of events from changes in properties of theories that generate hypotheses about these events. Still, some useful dichotomization of this sort is possible. Section 1.2 concerns some important changes in perceptions of events, all analysed in some depth in later chapters. Section 1.3 concerns some important changes in theory, all analysed later on in the book.

Moving along roughly the sequential plan of the book, *banking* looks nothing like it once did. Banks used to be perceived as more or less passive depositories that lent out funds entrusted to them. Big modern banks are propelled by an asset-based dynamic: they seek out lending opportunities *anywhere* (the euro-currency explosion reflects a profound reorientation of global *financement*): then they seek to finance these acquisitions just as do other companies. The upshot produces statistics such as the *cause célèbre* of spring 1977: Citicorp derives 13 per cent of its earnings from Brazil! The highly international focus of big modern banks deeply saps a number of conventional notions about monetary policy: the stock of euro-dollars exceeds that of U.S.M-1, but the euro-dollar market largely is outside the regulatory ambit of the American authorities; the identification of *money* with *state money* (prevalent only since the time of the French Revolution) has become insecure as trading nexuses have become more complex; it has become increasingly anachronistic to stress holdings of sterling by British citizens or holdings of kroner by Norwegians, etc. The *money-supply-definition* perplex, always substantial, has become intensified and elaborated; money-supply theory looks more and more like a theory searching for a fact.

There has developed a triad of profound shifts in perception of cause-and-effect in the monetary policy sphere. The components include (i) money-growth, price-inflation and unemployment; (ii) the rate of money-growth and the rate of interest; (iii) money-growth and share prices. Suffice it to say that orthodoxy prevalent as recently as say 1965, surely (!) 1960, has got stood on its head in each instance. Informed perception today is that intensified monetary growth will push up the unemployment rate, that interest rates will rise if money-supply accelerates and that there is a negative correlation between inflation and share prices, not long ago deemed an excellent inflation hedge. Why?

Crowding out is a prime topic in the financial press; it was supposed to have been banished by Keynes's monumental *General Theory*, along with the Treasury View, celebrated in the still earlier Macmillan report. Now informed opinion is highly sensitive to the possibility of public spending choking off capital formation. True, one does not hear much about 'public affluence and private squalor'; one soon might though, just as one once did; the French Revolution of 1789, after all, impinged upon that theme.

Not many years ago *money-supply* attracted very little serious study and much derisive dismissal. Indeed the concept 'stock of money' was not operational in official British circles. There has been a total transformation of opinion pervading academic, governmental, banking and stock-market circles. The framework of the Federal Reserve's policy structure has shifted, significantly but far from completely, towards money-supply and away from 'money-market conditions'; publication, each Thursday afternoon, in the United States of weekly money-supply changes is eagerly awaited in Wall Street; these weekly figures, full of 'noise' as they are, have provoked a pseudo-science amongst Wall Street analysts.

There have been dramatic changes in the way *unemployment* is perceived; these changes have been accompanied by others in the field of theory, concerning how the unemployment rate may be affected by such 'controls' as money-supply, unemployment benefits, minimum wage levels, etc. As in a number of important instances, unemployment statistics tend to be broken down, *disaggregated*. Unemployment among heads of households is more serious than that among married women above the age of 45; high unemployment rates among school-leavers are partially discounted because of the effects of minimum-wage requirements, together with more generous 'dole' terms. It is generally recognized that the economic and psychological consequences of unemployment are less severe in a modern welfare state than they were years ago. And it is recognized that the *duration* of unemployment experiences is of importance comparable with the unemployment-rate statistic. A major consequence of all these changes in the perception of enemployment has been the placement of more stress on inflation.

Any detailed discussion of American *money-supply regimes* should be left to Chapter 3: some hints have been dropped here; the analysis tends to require intense concentration on many details. Money-supply control in Britain is at least as technically cumbersome as in America, but the state of play has changed so profoundly in Britain that a remark can be made here: after all, not many years ago, as we have said, money-supply was not an operational concept in British officialdom; today it is, very much so. *Res ipsa loquitur!*

The explosive growth of *euro-currency markets* has led to an internationalization of *financement* that would be incomprehensible to anyone whose experience terminated in, say, 1955; today, major borrowers make narrow calculations about the weights that they will give to various currencies in the 'currency bundles' they take off the market; indeed it is possible, effectively, to borrow one 'cocktail' of currencies and be obligated to repay with another. The 'euro markets' reflect, among other things, tremendous internationalization of business. Thus it no longer is clear in what sense a major American company is American: the cases of IBM, Ford, Eastman Kodak, Exxon, Standard Oil of California and such banks as Bank of America, Citibank, Chase Manhattan and Morgan are evocative but not exceptional. True, major companies in countries such as Sweden, Holland or Switzerland, typically too small to supply a home market large enough to justify immense overheads, have operated all over the world for a long time; the difference between them and postwar American internationally expanding companies is one of degree; but the matter of degree is important since contemporary American 'multi-nationals' often are so large that their investment and marketing decisions—taken at home—have a severe impact on the autarchical integrity of the countries in which they operate. *Autarchical integrity* has been sapped in the largest countries by the internationalization of financial and other markets; political frontiers, together with the concept of national sovereignty, remain well defined, but the economic events operating upon these 'sovereignties' are amorphous.

Share-price formation is perceived very differently in chastened stock markets than, say, in 1968. Few then would have believed that in 1977 there would be mutual funds (unit trusts) invested in *bonds* or that sophisticated, 'computerized' investment-management companies would promote funds 'indexed' to such averages as the 'S & P 500', merely acquiring securities so that their values would correspond to the Standard & Poor weights. And the notion of what is a *growth company* or a *growth stock* has much changed: in 1968 it sufficed not to pay cash dividends to enjoy a growth-stock 'multiple'; today the criteria seem to be shaped by the wizened bankers with green eye-shades of old Hollywood films. In no economic sphere has perception of what is happening been so much influenced by changing theories about what is happening as in the stock markets, especially in America and Britain. In particular, *random-walk* and *rational-expectations* theories have exerted powerful influence on the markets' 'vision' (cf. the discussion of 'Life as the Imitation of Art' later in Chapter 1).

Until well into the 1960s, it seemed obvious that *macro-economic growth*, as measured by Gross National Product or Gross Domestic Product was a good thing; the policy-exercise simply was to achieve the maximum feasible rate of economic growth subject, in Britain for example, to nagging balance-of-payments consequences if such growth was not 'export-led', as it hardly ever was. Only in the Communist countries, and not in all of them, is there such a consensus today. This shift in opinion has at least two facets: to some extent such factors as 'environment' and 'preservation' have made a deeper impression on opinion (cf.

Chapters 8 and 9 comprising *Economics and Ethics*); to some extent, as a disaggregative approach to the economy became increasingly dominant, GDP-type statistics simply looked less and less meaningful even from an unabashedly materialistic standpoint. Chapter 7 seeks to develop a disaggregated scheme for studying the macro-economy. In such a scheme, one can espy that the kind of economic growth promoted by bad weather that might lead to more electricity generation or by expansion of local-authority clerical employment should not be treated equivalently, as it *is* in the conventional national-income accounts, with growth in the numbers of books produced and sold or in cinema productions, etc. Another advantage of a disaggregated approach to the macro-economy lies in improved understanding of *less-developed economies;* the internationalization of business has led to intense practical concern about such economies, often key growth-points for many businesses. Once again our inherent inability to disentangle art from life, events from theories about them, is notable.

1.3 New Theories about Economic Events

By far the most important theoretical development reported here concerns *rational expectations.* The rational-expectations literature has fulfilled certain conjectures and somewhat discursive intensions of the great economist and moral philosopher, Frank Knight. In its leap towards high theory, economics lost sight of its inherently humanistic and social character; the great leap forward was based on mathematics and physics. Recent developments are not reactionary; it is not proposed to surrender ground that has properly been gained; rather, the implications of the particles of economics being sensate and intelligent are being much more deeply explored. The most important upshot roughly is this:

> Without breaching the thicket containing the problem of whether *any* phenomenon can have existence independently of our perception of it (cf. Bishop Berkeley!), there seems to be an important sense in which the parameters controlling the motions of the particles of physics are invariant against formation by experimenters of theories about them and of plans to conduct experiments on the particles. The particles of economics cannot properly be assumed thus to be inanimate. The parameters controlling *their* behaviour will be in what may be a symbiotic linkage with the experimenters, e.g. the Board of Governors of the Federal Reserve and the British Chancellor.

The thrust of the fascinating workings out of this new/old approach to economics has, in the field of *stabilization policy*, been inhibitory: it becomes much harder to conceive that 'stabilizing' policies reduce amplitudes of economic fluctuations in many cases; in other instances, it is easy to see how such policies could make the economy more turbulent. Obviously, the 'rational-expectations' movement encourages support for secularly-orientated policies like the monetary rule associated with Professor Milton Friedman.

The impact of the new research on such subjects as securities markets and industrial organization has been substantial, but less revolutionary: *game theory*, at least as far back as the great work of von Neumann and Morgenstern in 1944, already had much influenced thinking in these areas, and along rather the same lines. So it is not surprising that there now is little support for the idea that one can make money in securities mostly because the markets do not know what they are doing; contained in this perception is the forecast that stock markets do not possess dumb-beast reflexes so that they spurt up because governments initiate inflationary programmes. As for 'industrial organization' in the broadest sense, the discussion in Chapter 9 of 'internalization of external diseconomies' (an upstream paper mill, releasing noxious effluvia into a river, upon acquiring affected downstream properties, operates the globalized sub-economy efficiently) warns us against neglecting study of the subtle and complex ways in which rational property owners will, if permitted by governments, be led by selfish (egoistic) motivation into efficient resource-use. The upshot has been almost a whole new subject, *law-and-economics*.

There have been other important, if less dramatic, developments in economic theory with portent for policy. Some of these have already been referred to. The theory of unemployment has been much enriched by simple applications from the theory of gases! The theory of money, banking and finance has finally become properly integrated. Statistical applications, including spectral analysis, have become remarkably more powerful as computer applications have deepened. One of the most interesting developments in economics in recent years has centred on *information;* Professors Stigler and Arrow are indelibly associated with a new, but now large, literature concerning search-costs, decisions on how much information to accumulate and how thoroughly to process it relative to costs, etc. The resulting amended *decision theory* is not amendable to classical statistics; there has, as a result, been tremendous development of what is called Bayesian statistical theory (named after yet another ordinand of the inexhaustibly eccentric Church of England). As a result, another push towards its properly humanistic–social territory has been imparted to economics. True, the costs of obtaining data and processing it affect designs of physical experiments, but in economics the 'particles' under study conduct the equivalents to experiments and then plan optimizing conduct relative to their results; the economist, the observer of these 'particles' and the work they do, must take account of the fact that the 'particles' he observes are selecting their data spaces! When these new developments in decision theory are combined with rational-expectations theory, the symbiosis including the experimenters (policy makers) and the things they study becomes complete. The ontological implications for economic science of its indeterminate data-base must be passed over here: it suffices to say that the distance between economics and physics looks greater and greater as economists think more deeply about their subject.

1.4 Ethics and Economics: Some Themes

Part III, *Economics and Ethics,* hinges most importantly on the distinction between the way in which we can *know* that the middle term of a syllogism is undistributed and that in which it can be *revealed* to us that political dissidents in Russia should be supported or that the press should be free. And, unlike Parts I and II which are quite free-standing, Part III is just the top of an iceberg whose mass has been built up over many years, in ways that did not seem to me, until recently, to have anything to do with economic policy. Three themes have been especially important to me and, to my surprise, did much to shape Chapter 8 in particular: Tradition and the Individual Talent; Fate and Fault; Life as the Imitation of Art.

1.4.1 Tradition and the Individual Talent

>   ... *What is to be insisted upon is that the poet must develop or procure the consciousness of the past and that he should continue to develop this consciousness throughout his career.*
>   *What happens is a continual surrender of himself as he is at the moment to something which is more valuable...*
>   T. S. Eliot, *Tradition and the Individual Talent, Selected Essays: 1917–1932* (New York: Harcourt, Brace & Co.; 1932), pp. 6–7

> *Time present and time past*
> *Are both perhaps present in time future,*
> *And time future contained in time past.*
> *If all time is eternally present*
> *All time is unredeemable.*

T. S. Eliot, *Burnt Norton,* appearing in *Four Quartets* (New York: Harcourt, Brace & Co.; 1943), p. 3.

The reader of Chapter 8 will recognize how this material got cast up in its passages on 'the State as the Guardian of Continuity'. Nor can I deny that other writers exerting powerful influence upon me—Thomas Mann, Kafka, Joyce, Proust, Hemingway *et al.*—were highly sensitive to their role as *artist* sojourning in some place at some time but not vitally of any particular place, at any special time. At the least, it is impossible for me to accept libertarian formulations of freedom of possessively-individualist material choice as the supreme criterion for policy. True, inborn scepticism about the ability of human action to improve the human condition—together with observation of *so much* counterproductive intervention—makes me pull back from the furthermost implications of this cast of mind.

1.4.2 Fate and Fault

Was it the *fault* of Oedipus, or simply his *fate?* Lear was so foolish, but he was a *king;* could such a fate for a king be the consequence of so squalid a fault? Nor has it ever been possible for me to define the properties of right actions. I do not *know* what are my moral duties, or yours.

In law these conundrums never have been resolved. True, one can say, in a way that is not trivial, 'law is not justice'. But the equity branch of the law, derived from the Chancellor's courts and rife with natural-law and canon-law concepts, makes categorical dissociation of 'law' from 'justice' chimerical: one wants to be Austinian, but it never proves feasible to be so.

Many economists make much less modest claims. They seem to *know*, as Pigou, admittedly rather diffidently, seemed to know, that equality is better than inequality or that it is *wrong* to force people to abstain from consumptions they like. I do not *know* any of these things. Nor do I think I can know such things. Indeed I long ago ceased to strive for such things: after much effort, I abandoned hope of learning what are the proper bounds of individual freedom from J. S. Mill's *On Liberty;* he clearly did not *know;* I found I. A. Richards's books on criticism wonderful, but Richards did not *know* what was a good poem. Chapters 8 and 9 are meant to inure the reader to the stern limitations of economics as a guide to knowledge of the right action. Economics is a useful, but pedestrian, subject—neither Prince Hamlet nor meant to be.

1.4.3 Life as the Imitation of Art

Two experiences, one more mundane than the other, wrenched me away from any notion that art operated on material comprising life, that the artist and the material he worked with were not in a symbiosis. Of course, once one is convinced that art and life are in a symbiotic relationship, it is a short step to acceptance that the behaviour of particles operated on by economic policy makers cannot properly be deemed independent of the forms of the 'experiments' that in fact cannot be made *on* them.

The less mundane experience flowed from Graham Greene's play, *The Living Room* (New York: The Viking Press; 1954). Father James Browne is an intellectual priest who long has ached to play a pastoral role. His inept attempts to do so lead to a suicide. Will not some of the play's readers, when placed in similar positions, imitate Father Browne, perhaps sado-masochistically? How many men have played Charles Swann *vis-à-vis* girls who otherwise would be nothing like Odette Crécy?

The more mundane experience is in some ways more evocative. Does Provence look the way it does because that is the way it looks or because Cézanne and Van Gogh painted Provençal scenes as they did, indelibly moulding our perception? Indeed these remarkable achievements are *not* mundane. Even less so were others of Cézanne who paved the way for the cubism of Picasso and Braque *et al.* that so completely altered our 'innate' conceptions of spatial relationships. These monumental accomplishments in painting evoke quite directly a theme that flits through the book: acts of perception create that which appears to be perceived. That abstract notion, 'the economy', is as much the creation of economic theory as it is its field of study.

Part I Finance

Part 1 Finance

2 The Logic of Money and Finance

2.1 Introduction to Chapter 2

2.1.1 Conception of Chapter 2

Chapter 2 is more concerned with finance than money; it is much more concerned with lending and borrowing than with how debts get extinguished or with the nature of substances ordinarily tendered against debt.

Think of Economies A and B. In A no trader gives or takes credit overnight or longer; what is bought during today is paid for today with unborrowed resources. There is no lending or borrowing in A; A's simple economy does not require a theory of finance. A's economy does provoke monetary theory: what objects are tendered against debt, measured in 'money of account'? Such objects will be called *money*. B has a financial as well as a monetary system; there is lending and borrowing in B. Some claims used to extinguish debt in B may have been generated by acts of *financement*: banks will have bought assets by issuing cashier's cheques that became deposited in the banking system. Such assets include loan-stock issued by businesses expanding their inventories (stocks): bank depositors may thus have increased their net wealth, this being balanced by real wealth embodied in newly created business inventories. Such a coincidence between *financement* and growth in the B money-stock would not be vital for a theory of money; the logic of B's debt-discharge arrangements would be the same if its money stock had been generated as follows.

B's Treasury retired Government debt held by the public, simultaneously selling tap stock to the central bank. So the banks' central-bank credit increased, leading them to expand their assets until bank-deposits regained their normal, multiplied, relation to bank-held central-bank credit. The public would be induced to alter its collective balance sheet, exchanging non-monetary for monetary assets; the process would not concern *financement* of cash-deficits by cash-surpluses.

13

Financement and *money* are quite different in B.

The clearing (commercial) banks are at the interface of money and finance and so bulk large in the chapter. In a perfectly stationary economy, the clearing banks would be mere chequeries; nor are clearing banks preponderantly intermediaries between savers and borrowers in the real world. Banks play a savings-intermediary role only to the extent that money-supply expansions are accompanied by concomitant expansions of *real* monetary assets; banks may finance additional working capital, buying commercial paper balanced by deposit-increments.

In the real world changes in the volume of central-bank credit displace clearing banks from equilibrium. The efforts of banks to regain portfolio-balance perturbate the securities markets. So, at least transitorally, the processes by which 'real' savings finance 'real' investments will be importantly affected by behaviour in the central bank/clearing bank nexus.

2.1.2 The Work of Chapter 2

Lending and borrowing in modern economies are preponderantly indirect. Why? Mostly because of liquidity- and safety-motives of households and the technology governing placement of the vast tranches of financial capital required by the huge companies dominating modern economies.

The chapter first considers the importance of *financial mediation,* producing intermediate paper. Then it turns to the reserve structure of the financial sector, yielding 'The Controlling Principle of Banking Theory'. The Principle breaks open *financial disintermediation and re-intermediation* as well as seemingly remote subjects like *euro-dollars.* Then *clearing banks* are studied. It is hard to generalize about modern clearing banks: the *asset-orientation* of Citicorp or Morgan must be contrasted with the *liability-orientation* of typical local banks.

The pieces comprising the financial sector being in place, Central Banking and Monetary Policy' can be elaborated. It is established that liquidity dislocations *indirectly* transmit central-bank actions to the 'real' economy. The underlying theory is firmly embedded in economics: demanders and suppliers in *competitive markets* respond to prices, not to total availabilities (probably unknown) of the products they deal in; if a supply curve shifts, perhaps because of a crop failure, the price will rise; the change in the supply-condition may not be otherwise perceived.

The ether transmitting the impulses of monetary policy is composed of demands for and supplies of the myriad money-market instruments; it is agitated by liquidity-dislocations; securities prices are perturbed.

Inflation expectations also affect securities prices. In recent years Irving Fisher's conjectures about *inflation expectations and interest rates* have been expanded and deepened. There are many ramifications: when interest rates go up, perhaps the real cost of borrowing is increasing; it may be decreasing! What are the *expectations* about prices of goods and services in future? The analysis must needs be murky: expectations cannot be observed.

Another ramification concerns *share prices*. In an extended 'Fisherine' analysis, the relationships between share-prices and interest-rates are subjective: if inflation-expectations become ignited, interest rates will go up, along with expected profits—perhaps! Indeed the theory of share-price formation (cf. Chapter 6) comprises a multi-dimensional vortex. The idea of *efficient markets* is linked to *rational expectations*. Efficient-market hypotheses hold that a stock market somehow absorbs all relevant information and then correctly assesses it relative to the most powerful available theory. One cannot hope to beat such a market.

Stock markets, efficient or not, determine the *cost of capital*. And share prices, defining the cost of equity capital, are affected by interest rates: theories of stock markets and of central banking are symbiotic.

The chapter concludes with an analysis of *central banks and real rates of interest*. Finally enough material will have been accumulated to permit perception of the dense network of analytic threads linking up the nodes of the whole economy, 'real' and financial.

It is impossible to distinguish *monetary theory* from *income theory;* Chapter 2, as it rushes on, floods much ground habitually occupied by Chapter 7.

Is there a trade-off between public spending and private capital-formation? If so, what are its terms? Once *crowding out* is grasped, it is easy to describe *fully-employed* economies. The description encompasses *involuntary unemployment* of labour and other productive resources. And another concept must be elaborated *en parallèle: the natural rate of unemployment*.

All this work culminates in the *natural rate of interest* idea. We want to distinguish acutely between what is feasible and what is infeasible for central banks to do. If an economy is operating at effectively full employment—the requirements are not stringent—the central bank cannot drive down the *real* rate of interest; if it tries to do so, inflation will accelerate. If an economy is not operating near an effectively-full employment-level, the central bank *can* depress prevailing interest rates.

Chapters 3 and 4 concern modalities of money-supply control in the U.S. and U.K., thus ornamenting the abstract development of Chapter 2.

Chapter 3 centres on the odd way in which the Federal Reserve supplies credit to, or drains credit from, the system with an eye on federal-funds rate. Chapter 4 centres on consequences for money-supply behaviour of the wide range of assets eligible to satisfy reserve requirements against British bank deposits: the expansion-rate of

British money-supply has become responsive to loan-demand. Indeed, as British authorities have become senstitive to the ways in which British money-supply is apt to move sympathetically with 'the needs of trade', they have issued supplementary, quite clotted, regulations, including the 'Corset'.

2.2 The Indirectness of Modern Financement; Asset Switching and Real Saving, Lending, and Hence Borrowing, in Advanced Economies

Lending, and hence borrowing, in advanced economies mostly is indirect; lending/borrowing mostly is done through financial intermediaries. The *raison d'être* of mediation has two facets. One concerns safety; the other, liquidity.

Only eccentrics keep large amounts of bearer paper, currency, e.g. at home. And the *first* bankers lent out metals left with them for safe-keeping: the safety motive induces indirect *financement*.

The liquidity, or fungibility, property has at least two sub-properties: suitability for portfolio investment; efficiency in debt settlement.

It is much easier to encash a bank account, an insurance policy or a listed security than the note of a private person (even if guaranteed by a famous house), a mortgage, etc. The explanation importantly contains *transactions costs:* think of one's search for a buyer of unlisted paper. Financial intermediation massively reduces such costs.

Preponderantly face-to-face debt settlement today would be inefficient when not futile. Keynes wrote, so felicitously, about how Pope's father went into retirement with a cruse, full of coins. In a modern economy, increasingly dominated by computer-aided signalling, account-settlement has become so 'remote' as transactions nexuses have expanded and bookkeeping has become electronically controlled, that a massive hoard of coins would be extremely non-liquid for almost any transactor. So the modern transactor is further impelled towards lending his funds to financial intermediaries who will lend them to non-financial borrowers.

There are other compelling reasons for financial mediation. Real-estate developers would not find it feasible to fund multi-million dollar projects through small individual subscriptions. Vast companies such as Sears or Marks & Spencer make up their borrowed working capital, financing vast inventories (stocks), with large credit tranches; it would be inefficient for them to seek small loans! Indirect *financement* is imbedded in advanced economies and becomes more predominant as the economy advances.

2.2.1 Household Balance Sheets

Households own large amounts of government and limited-company (corporate) securities. 'Prudence' and 'liquidity' especially favour central-government debt, riskless, in Communist countries at least, save for unthinkable political possibilities: central governments operate printing presses. Listed corporate securities are highly liquid: markets are made for them on stock exchanges; safety can be enhanced through diversification. Still, most household financial assets are claims against financial institutions, including pension trusts. Household financial liabilities support consumer-durable holdings, including houses and cars. These liabilities comprise the assets of building societies and like institutions.

Household balance sheets are functions of the age of the head-of-household. Young persons typically have negative net cash flow as they accumulate indebtedness. Middle-aged persons typically accumulate financial assets on net, building up the nest-eggs that will finance old age. What is important to see here is that household balance sheets interact through intermediate transactions with financial institutions; such transactions are far more important than household-to-household dealings.

A substantial portion of the assets and liabilities of households are not reflected by any financial instrument; this portion comprises the imputed relations with the public sector. Social-security rights—old-age-pension and unemployment-insurance rights, etc.—are household assets, just as expected tax obligations are liabilities.

The asset/liability structures of households *vis-à-vis* the public sector are highly sensitive to age. Elderly and retired workers have strongly positive imputed positions; unmarried, young skilled workers must anticipate large tax payments towards support of pensioners for many years.

Defence poses knotty problems for social accountants. In one sense defence is worth more, over lifetime horizons, to younger than to older people: the expected stream of defence, like refuse-collection, benefits is longer for younger people. But defence, and other social services, have a qualitative dimension: elderly persons too are exigent about their security. Tax liability for defence is easier to handle: the present value of defence-related tax liability varies directly with age, *everything else the same*.

The sketch of household balance sheets shows that *everybody* is to some degree a capitalist; each manages a portfolio of assets and liabilities, with varying amounts of discretion. The universal category of economic actors is *capitalist*. And it follows that another universal category is *risk-taker*. Thus currency is a risky asset: it is vulnerable to the inflation-rate.

2.2.2 Duality of Financial Assets and Liabilities

Financial-asset and *financial-liability* are dual concepts. The concepts are rooted in debt and so link lending and borrowing. So the assets of financial intermediaries are comprised either of the debts of the private and public sectors or of claims against the private sector in the form of share-ownership; the financial assets of the non-financial private sector include the liabilities of the financial sector. The matted tangle of financial relationships in an advanced economy, requiring intricate netting-out calculations before sectoral net-positions can be computed, results from the characteristically *indirect* financial dealings between transactors in advanced systems.

Balance sheets display the accumulated consequences of transactions performed over an indefinite past. Some transactions reflect acts of saving in the sense of abstinence from consumption by households or retained earnings by companies. Others have nothing to do with saving. Consider the liabilities of a savings bank or building society. Some of the funds that flowed into such an institution corresponded with savings, at least in the sense that these flows corresponded with resources becoming available for investment. Other funds simply resulted from balance-sheet switching; proceeds of share-sales may have been put into savings banks.

It follows that

the processes determining savings of real resources are not reflected in any simple way by flows into 'savings' institutions. 'Savings' inflows may be offset by dissaving: durables may have been allowed to deteriorate. Withdrawals from savings accounts may pay for courses building up 'human capital'. Or 'savings' inflows may result from *re-intermediation*.

And that

central banks do not supply real resources; central banks do affect liquidity conditions.

The difference between actions operating on *liquidity* and those operating on *wealth* is important and hard to grasp. Central-banking theory would be easy if central-bank actions predominantly affected rationally-perceived wealth. Then accelerated money-growth would stimulate expenditure plans; at 'full employment', inflation would have to accelerate for spending plans to become reconciled to supply constraints; the growth-rate of real money-balances would be brought down into conformity with the maximum feasible growth-rate of real output by the higher inflation-rate. Reality is different. The *duality* of financial assets and liabilities prevents central-bank asset-purchases, leading to expansion of both sides of bank balance sheets, from generating wealth effects. If such a sequence has 'real' consequences, it will transmit impulses to the 'real' economy through its effects on asset (liability) prices.

We note, by way of a concluding ancillary comment, that central banks can be merchant (investment) banks as well. Recall the early days of the Bank of England or the First and Second Banks of the United States. In some less-developed countries today, central banks are merchant banks too. Equivalent processes occur in developed countries, but not through direct central-bank activity: thus the immense portion of the Italian industrial sector under public ownership and control essentially obtains its finance from the state.

2.3 The Reserve Structure of the Financial Sector

2.3.1 Preliminary Remarks

Each component of the financial sector perceives differently what happens to it and what it does.

Macro-economic events are exogenous to the biggest banks.

Central banks think the field of macro-economic data responds to their actions. There is a trivial sense in which this certainly is true: the members of the economy do not do what they do in order to change the actions of the central bank; the central bank does what it does to influence the public. Indeed *some* autonomy subsists in a central bank, even after exhausive analysis of feedback, the 'open' systems brought about by the development of the euro-dollar market (cf. Chapter 5), etc. Still the central bank's potential ability to influence the economy in desired ways can become nullified in at least two ways.

(1) The central bank may be operating under an invalid hypothesis; it may not be able to exert some influence it thinks it can or this influence may be different from what the bank thinks it is.
(2) The central bank may be collecting the wrong data relative to its hypotheses or its measurements may be inaccurate.

No region in the 'action space' of central banks is harder to comprehend than that occupied by *reserve structures*. It is difficult to formulate correct reserve-structure models and it is equally difficult to operate these models properly.

In order to fix ideas, we shall orientate development of the theory of reserve structures towards those perturbations in the matrix of claims leading to financial disintermediation and re-intermediation, in turn pointing up distinctions between clearing banks that are members of the Federal Reserve System (or its equivalent) and other financial institutions, including clearing banks that are not.

Excluding *currency drain*—conversion of deposits into currency—the central-bank-credit component of member-bank reserves cannot be drained off. And, since other asset/liabilities that might be treated as reserves, liquid assets, etc. can be generated within the system (endogenously), central-bank credit then would determine member-bank deposit-liability in a system in which the Bank exercised remorseless control of its credit-emission. Then the aggregate deposits of member banks would be determined by total central-bank credit; the aggregate deposit liability of 'the rest' simply would reflect demand.

The ways in which central banks try, and sometimes fail, to control deposit liabilities will be studied in Chapter 3. Here we centre on implications of a model in which central-bank credit, once pumped into the system (into the member banks, the only eligible creditors), can be drained off only by the Bank. And facile exposition requires that we assume that *all clearing banks are member banks*.

2.3.2 Preliminary survey of essential properties of reserve-management

Obviously, an economy can be broken down into *clearing banks* (Sector B), *non-clearing banks whose liabilities are subject to cheque* (Sector $\bar{B}$) and *the rest* (Sector C).

Any member, b_i, of B holds its reserves, surely its required reserves, as central-bank credit. Only members of B are to own central-bank credit.

In order to obtain symmetry in 'fiducial reputation', assume that $\bar{b}_j$, a member of $\bar{B}$, spends cheques on B as they come in, just as b_i spends cheques on $\bar{B}$ as soon as *they* come in.

C owns short-dated claims, including deposits, against B and $\bar{B}$.

Currency is ignored.

Profit-Maximizing Behaviour Upon b_i crediting a customer with the face amount of a cheque drawn by him against a member of $\bar{B}$ (henceforth, 'against $\bar{B}$'), b_i's assets and liabilities will have increased by the same amount. b_i will want to convert this claim against $\bar{B}$ immediately for at least two reasons: its reserve-requirement will be greater because of the fresh deposit; b_i will want to make new loans and investments, paying for fresh assets with cashier's cheques. Any cheque paid into b_q will be cleared at the Bank against b_i; b_i must convert his claim against $\bar{B}$ into Bank credit.

An institutional rubric should be supplied.

b_i is entitled to demand currency from $\bar{B}$ under the legal-tender act. So $\bar{b}_s$ gladly agrees to supply central-bank-credit potential to b_i by writing a sight-draft against a member of B. The modalities suggest that $\bar{b}_s$ will want to maintain B balances—in order to minimize transactions costs; $\bar{b}_s$ always can sell assets for B-claims.

$\bar{B}$ If $\bar{b}_j$ receives a cheque drawn on b and does not wish to accumulate

B-claims, $\bar{b}_j$ will acquire assets from C, drawing a draft on b_i. (Members of C would accept payment in B or $\bar{B}$ funds.)

The $\bar{B}$ balance-sheet contracts in the aftermath of a $\bar{B}$ claim falling into B hands; the B balance sheet does not contract if a B claim falls into $\bar{B}$ hands. The $\bar{B}$ balance-sheet expands if a B claim falls into $\bar{B}$ hands; the B balance-sheet does not expand if a $\bar{B}$ claim falls into B hands. The *aggregate* balance-sheet of B is determined by the volume of central-bank credit; that of $\bar{B}$ by 'demand'.

C C is assumed simply not to want more currency. Assume further that c_k wants to reduce his B-account; he will draw a cheque on B in payment say for securities. Since B alone has central-bank credit-opportunity, unwanted B-credit simply will bounce about the system—until there is a macro-economic resolution.

What if c_k wants to reduce his $\bar{B}$-credit? A crucial asymmetry, rooted in the reserve-system will become displayed. A cheque against $\bar{b}_j$, drawn by c_k, is to be paid into b_i. $\bar{b}_j$ must find B-funds; $\bar{b}_j$ must sell assets, presumably dipping into his liquid reserves and then replenishing them by sales of other assets. $\bar{B}$'s assets and liabilities will have fallen. *Thus disintermediation!*

Recapitulation through a new form of analysis The analysis can be put into *Markov chains*.

The *matrix of claims* transists each instant. The reserve position of B perpetually is in an absorbing state; it perpetually transists into itself. Each time a cheque against $\bar{B}$ is received in B, $\bar{B}$ must liquidate assets; lower levels of desired claims against $\bar{B}$ induce transitions so that the new equilibrium—i.e. absorbing—state finds $\bar{B}$'s assets and liabilities correspondingly shrunken. Each time a cheque against B is received in $\bar{B}$, *no* change occurs in equilibrium magnitudes of B assets and liabilities.[1]

Currency Drain Currency·drain can be put aside; the stipulations about required-reserve ratios for clearing banks and the fact that only clearing banks have central-bank credit are sufficient to establish that clearing banks cannot be drained of required reserves by transactors and that their equilibrium deposit-levels are determined simply by the volume of bank credit.

Currency drain admittedly blurs the argument's lines. To the extent that currency might comprise clearing-bank reserves, currency-withdrawals would drain off clearing-bank reserves; clearing-bank holdings of central bank credit cease to be autonomous. Still, clearing banks are not *characteristically* drained of their reserves when depositors wish to reduce their claims against them. Thus compare clearing banks with savings banks whose deposits are subject to cheque. Such deposits may be prime means of payment. Still savings-bank liquidity will be squeezed by net withdrawals: withdrawals in favour of clearing banks become settled in a way generating a clearing-bank claim against the central bank. The savings bank would have to find currency, make securities sales or draw down its own deposits.

Withdrawals from clearing banks in favour of savings banks do not reduce the former's *aggregate* central-bank credit. Nor would it matter if B̄ insisted upon being paid in B̄-funds: extinguishment of a B-deposit creates excess B-demand for assets (reflecting excess sector reserves) 1:1; as B̄ buys assets with its fresh deposits, B̄ cashier cheques flow onto the market 1:1; required B̄-funds become generated spontaneously. In the process's final equilibrium, the market will *want* to hold the B-funds that splashed onto it so that B̄-funds could be acquired. The price of B̄-funds in terms of B-funds will be constant so long as sectoral solvencies are assured; price-adjustment will occur among securities substitutional with B- or B̄-funds. (In our example there initially is excess demand for such securities.)

The argument has hinged upon what can be called an 'immunity property'. Clearing banks, stipulated all to be member banks, are *immune* from drain of central-bank credit, comprising required reserves. The immunity-property is converse to the 'required reserve' property; the properties, taken together, assure that aggregate clearing-bank deposit-liability depends on the volume of central-bank credit and not on the condition of demand for such deposits.

In logical terms, and where z = the 'immunity property', A = the set of companies with central-bank credit, $\bar{A}$ = the reciprocal of A, and B = the clearing banks, the necessary and sufficient conditions for B and B alone to possess an equilibrium-level of deposit-liability independent of 'demand'—given the required-reserve property—are

$$B = A$$

since

$$z \in A$$

in the sense that z appertains to A and

$$z \cap \bar{A} = 0$$

in the sense that z does not appertain to $\bar{A}$.

Exposition of the 'Controlling Proposition of Banking Theory' has opened up *disintermediation* and *re-intermediation*.

2.4 Financial Disintermediation and Re-intermediation

'Disintermediation' logic boils down to these propositions.

(1) Increased preference for the liabilities of a company, not a clearing bank (all clearing banks being 'member banks'), in favour of some other company, not a clearing bank, has no effect on the overall state of excess demand in credit markets. The upshot is neither disintermediation nor re-intermediation.

(2) Increased preference on net for the liabilities of clearing banks makes for disintermediation and excess demand for short-securities, i.e. 'tighter money'.

(3) Decreased preference on net for clearing-bank liabilities makes for re-intermediation and excess supply of short-securities, i.e. 'easier money'.

Look at examples of the three cases.

(1) Households want to reduce their building-society deposits by $X and to buy $X in newly issued private-sector bonds. Companies plan to reduce bank-indebtedness with the proceeds. The building societies will sell assets, perhaps reducing their claims against banks, thus raising $X. The households simply will have switched assets; the companies will have switched liabilities. The banks will have excess liquidity unless they find alternative loan- and investment-placements: they might buy the assets sold by the building societies or acquire assets from those who bought building-society assets.

Generalizing case (1), it finds contractions on both sides of building-society balance sheets accompanying a change in the form of corporate debt. Household credits have been transferred to the company-sector from the building societies. The latter have sold assets previously supported by this credit to, say, the banks who thus replaced credits repaid by the companies. True, some measures of money-supply will show decreases; these decreases will be factitious, since the changes in the claims-matrix merely reflect equilibrated changes in desired portfolios.

(2) Life-insurance-policy holders wish to reduce cash values of their policies and to buy time deposits from clearing banks with the proceeds. At first the insurance companies may reduce their bank balances; effects of differential reserve requirements relative to the new deposit mix being neglected, the upshot will not affect bank liquidity. The policy holders will be satisfied. But the insurance companies will be out of equilibrium: proportions borne by their short-assets to their long-assets will have fallen. The insurance companies will offer long-assets for cash; there will be no buyers until long-asset prices are marked down.

Case (2) demonstrates *disintermediation*. The net liabilities of financial institutions (more generally, 'certain transactors') will have fallen, together with their assets. Counterpart transactors (policy holders) conversely will have increased their assets and liabilities by the same amount that measures the contraction of the aggregate balance-sheet of non-banking financial institutions. Disequilibration of insurance-company balance sheets will have led to excess supply of long assets and excess demand for short assets.

The process is called *disintermediation* because analysts normally emphasize the short-term liabilities of financial institutions: insurance-company liabilities will have fallen. This usage is flawed; the important thing is that there develops net excess supply of long assets and excess demand for short assets. This key result follows upon encashment of claims against *anyone*, provided that the claimant intends to use the proceeds to increase his claims against clearing banks.

Generalizing case (2), it concerns incompatible plans. Policy holders want to increase their clearing-bank deposits more than insurance companies want to reduce theirs. The impasse can be resolved only by lower prices for long-assets, assuming that demand thus would be stimulated, or by re-intermediation.

(3) Depositors decide to reduce their claims against clearing banks, and to buy commercial paper like that issued by car-finance houses. Assuming, conveniently, that there are uniform reserve requirements against bank-liabilities, bank liquidity will be unaffected. But short assets will be in excess supply; there will be net excess demand for long assets and excess supply of short assets. Case (3) displays *re-intermediation* because it generates increased short-liabilities for non-banking financial intermediaries. This stress is misplaced just as it was in the disintermediation case, Case (2).

The generalization of case (3) is at hand from case (2). Case (3) is like 'musical chairs': someone always will be holding unwanted cash until a systematic resolution is found.

2.4.1 Afterword on disintermediation

Marginal effort will expose another controlling proposition, concerning the transmission of impulses generated by monetary policy to the 'real' economy.

It might seem that we have avoided an obvious solution to the problem of case (3):

> Undesired cash will be offered for goods, leading to increased real income and higher prices. Nominal national income will rise just enough to make transactors want to hold the 'excess' cash; higher incomes will induce demand for more cash.

This 'solution' is improper. Although the matrix-of-claims was perturbed, there were no effects on net wealth; there was no 'micro' incentive to increase spending on goods.

Assume that the finance companies successfully placed their fresh resources. These placements may have been at the expense of other such companies, but we are especially interested in the possibility that the fresh resources flowed into an expanding car-finance market.

If the car-finance market expanded along with the economy, the re-intermediation impulse simply would become absorbed by an expanding economy. Then the Federal Reserve might reduce the rate of expansion of the monetary base. The idea of an expanding system both deepens and simplifies the analysis.

Economists have assumed that monetary assets (liabilities) not offset by debt such as treasury currency—'outside money'—are treated by the public as net wealth. But currency is not net social wealth: only an *irrational* public would see it as such.

2.5 Modern commercial banking

Central- and clearing-banks are inextricably linked. Thus central banks operate on clearing-bank liquidity. The 'Controlling Proposition of Banking Theory' anticipates this result: only the clearing banks hold the great bulk of their reserves as central-bank credit.

Banking practice varies over the world. British and French banking are dominated by a few companies. American banking is much more diversified: many of the thousands of small American banks, protected by legislation blocking nationwide banking, are locally dominant; large American companies are approached by banks located all across the country. German banks have massive equity interests in German companies; American banks are prohibited from share-ownership, etc.

Still, world banking can be dichotomized.

The first category, containing most local and many regional American banks, for example, has a *deposit-dynamic* or a *liability-orientation principle*. Call these 'L banks'.

The second category, containing such money-centre banks as Citicorp and First Chicago and some regional banks, has an *asset dynamic* or an *asset-orientation principle*. Call these 'A banks'.

L banks do not aggressively sell *certificates of deposit* (CDs). And, for the most part, they supply *federal funds*. Their loan-demand flows from a stable set of clients and rises and falls sympathetically with the impact of the business-cycle in the various localities. So long as the deposit-growth of L banks roughly corresponds with the growth-path of their loan-demand, L banks simply alter the proportion of their loans to their investments (in gilt-edged stock, municipal bonds and the like) over the course of the cycle; loans become more important in mature business expansions for example.

Deposit- and loan-growth in L banks tends to be strongly positively correlated. Think of the American southwest. The thrust of the American economy towards the 'sunbelt' brought the deposits, as well as the loan-demand, of the firms and households coming out there.

L banks are glad to receive additional deposits; interest rates on time deposits typically are well below yields on open-market paper of comparable maturity. Promotional campaigns aim at attracting such 'resources'. For L banks, deposit-expansion is the proper engine of growth; growth through purchased funds is thought abnormal or imprudent.

Costs of purchased funds *are* volatile. Summer 1974 in the U.S. pointed up the dangers of buying short-term funds to support longer-term lending. Effective costs of short-term borrowing sometimes exceeded 14 per cent. Some banks that clumsily had tried to shift from an 'L' to an 'A' mode looked unable to roll over enough of their short debt to avoid failure. A number of failures were averted only by special help from the Federal Reserve. In Britain the situation was perhaps less publicized but was more serious still. British 'secondary' banks became undermined. There were some failures and many rescue operations (sometimes called 'lifeboat' operations) as it became irrefragably clear that long assets, such as real property, cannot prudently be financed by short-term paper sales.

When L banks are in their natural mode, deposit-growth leads and asset-growth follows.

The A/L dichotomization sometimes becomes fuzzy. Bank of America and the giant British banks are hybrids relative to the dichotomization: they have immense, highly-stable deposit bases. As a result, their prudential capital-funds requirements are relatively less than those of say the big Chicago banks, restricted to one-office banking in Illinois and heavily constrained within the U.S. by locally-biased banking laws. The dependence of the Chicago banks on purchased funds is all the greater relative to their growth strategies.

2.5.1 Intermezzo: clearing banks as financial intermediaries

Before analysing asset-orientated banks, we consider *clearing banks as financial intermediaries participating in the transmission of real resources from savers to capital-formation.*

When banks match increments to their retained earnings with new loans and investments, they are directly transmitting company savings. When banks sell investments to finance loans, they merely trade third-party paper with the public and so do not perform an intermediary function.

Any savings-intermediary role for clearing banks is imbedded in their special relationship with central banks. Consider an expansion of clearing-bank assets and liabilities concomitant with expanding central-bank credit reaching them. Clearing banks will exchange new liabilities (monetary assets, depending upon how *money* is defined) for non-monetary assets. A savings-intermediary role gets tacked on only to the extent that some savers want to increase their monetary assets concomitantly with the increase in central-bank-credit emission.

2.5.2 Conclusion of the A-bank analysis

It is easy to analyse banks operating on an *asset-based dynamic*. They seek investment opportunity everywhere and in anything they consider prudently attractive that will be approved by regulatory authorities. Final decisions will hinge on *risk as well as:* co-variance (i.e. meshing) of risks of possible ventures with those of initial portfolios is important, for example.

Incremental funds may be raised in many ways. New shares may be sold. Convertible bonds may be floated. But it is unlikely that freshets of spontaneous deposits will flow in just as substantial outlets for global resource deployment are uncovered. True, rough coincidence like this is possible: the huge money-centre banks attracted immense O.P.E.C. deposits after the increase in the oil-price in late 1973–1974. Still the principle is intact:

A banks as such simply sell their paper in the open market as do other companies expanding beyond the limits of their cash-flows. The new liabilities thus incurred do not include demand deposits; the expansion-process is outside their clearing-bank function.

The expansion of Citibank, Morgan, Chase Manhattan, Bank of America *et al.* into South America, Asia, Africa, etc. thus is irrelevant to their cheque-clearing activity or demand-depository status.

Filling in the international aspect of A-bank expansion, lending-risk is dichotomized into *project-risk* and *country-risk*. Country risk concerns politically-based adversities such as expropriation, repudiation, exchange controls, punitive taxation or administrative discrimination as well as ways in which global economic fluctuations might have especially adverse effects for various countries regardless of politics. One can see why stock markets and others (including Dr Burns) have been concerned about balance-of-payments loans by money-centre banks, let alone peripheral banks stumbling into participations; balance-of-payments loans are peculiarly vulnerable to country-risk.

Country-risk for a given bank often is less substantial than a cursory look suggests. A bank's 'book' in Country X will include X-currency-denominated liabilities. Furthermore, country-risk varies directly with the length of the loan-portfolio. A very short-dated asset portfolio could be virtually immune from country risk. The banks claim that indeed they have very short 'asset books' in volatile countries.

2.5.3 Bank profits and monetary policy

Banks, seen as stock markets see companies, are affected only transitorily by central-bank decisions on the expansion of the monetary base.

The argument travels along two directions. One concerns the banking industry in comparative isolation. The other direction concerns banks and central-bank policy.

¯There is a close causal connection between the rate of expansion of central-bank credit and that of passively-acquired bank-liabilities. Contrast the way in which proceeds of a Federal Reserve open-market purchase passively enter into the banking system with the way in which the equivalent to a commercial-paper sale actively increases the liabilities and lending resources of a bank seller. So it might seem that banks normally should increase their deposits and assets per dollar of bank-capital more rapidly during periods of more-rapid expansion of central-bank credit. Then earnings per share would be doubly sensitive to the 'money growth cycle': higher interests rates, roughly associated with higher price-inflation, would make demand deposits still more profitable, reflecting generally improved 'spreads' between yields on earning assets and on purchased money; 'action' per share would increase in that assets and liabilities per share would increase. So earnings per share would increase. The notion is incorrect, but not chimerical.

An episode, beginning roughly in the late 1960s and culminating in 1974–75, exposes both the skeletal logic and the snares of bank-expansion in inflationary times. Bankers became promoters of their stocks. And nothing propels a stock faster than rapid, accelerating growth in per-share earnings, if *earnings-quality* is not obviously deteriorating. It was expedient to increase leverage on bank-capital; the 1972–74 acceleration of monetary expansion made this possible even for timid operators. So, by late Spring 1974, when most bank-stock prices crashed, balance sheets of large American banks had become very thin; ratios of capital to loans and of capital-plus-loan-loss-reserves to loan-loss exposure fell well below historical norms. Deposits, and assets, per share rose substantially. And the rot went deeper still. Credit-quality standards had eroded, as the Real Estate Investment Trust (R.E.I.T.) fiasco showed. The collapse of bank-share prices in 1974 was followed by serious concern for the solvency of the American banking system by late 1975. The pressures were intensified by the aftermath of the 1974 liquidity crisis, partly caused by growing awareness of deterioration in bank balance-sheets. The response of the Federal Reserve was dangerously delayed.

Conventionally-prudent lending standards were not fully restored in July 1977. The American bank-sector remained shadowed:

Exceptional sluggishness in demand for commercial-and-industrial loans, at least at New York, persisted through the first half of 1977 and led to disproportionate expansion of domestic consumer- and real-estate loans.

Balance of payment loans to less-developed countries and to

communist-bloc countries aroused concern. True, the early Rothschilds lent large sums to governments in the time of Napoleon the Great. But the Rothschilds enjoyed much closer political liaison with their debtors than the American banks have with theirs. Cf. Russia! And the House of Rothschild always has been much more an investment bank than a fiducial depository.

There also has been a rapid expansion of project loans to such developing countries as Brazil, Mexico, Formosa and Korea; in 1976 Citicorp obtained 13 per cent of its after-tax global profit from Brazil, accounting for 5 per cent of its assets. True, much of this lending is in local currencies, matched by borrowings in these currencies. And Brazil's prospects are dazzling. Mexico will become a large oil exporter. Still one asks, 'to what extent has sluggish U.S. loan demand led to accelerated international lending, responding to pressures to sustain earnings growth?'

Earnings of big American banks continued to command shrunken multiples in July 1977.

The narrative implies that the *earnings-growth-through-leverage* concept is not simply chimerical: for a time it can work all round; some safety-ratios were excessive. The correct analysis of the interaction of bank balance-sheets and profits and profits with central-bank policy will establish perspective.

We want to analyse a banking system maining roughly equilibrium leverage (gearing): deposits and loans are to grow *pari passu* with capital.

The capital of a non-financial company mostly takes physical form. The money-price of physical capital and nominal profits go up with inflation; under the practically unattainable stipulations required for balanced inflation, real rates of return, and the real cost of capital, would persist unchanged.

Bank capital mostly is embodied in money-fixed claims. If the terms of bank-loans have been negotiated so that running yields offset inflationary erosions of principal and income, banks will, to that extent, be in inflation-neutral postures.

If a bank's price-earnings ratio (p/e), its multiple, is to be invariant against expected inflation, then

> If leverage is constant, net interest income must increase relative to nominal capital (for banks, roughly equal to book capital) at the inflation rate.

Say that the after-tax real rate of interest is and is to remain at 3 per cent per annum and that the inflation-rate is 6 per cent: paper bought by banks would have to yield 9 per cent for the bank's multiple (i.e. the p/e of its shares) to be sustained. If it retained half its earnings, its capital would grow at 4·5 per cent per annum; it would sustain a 9 per cent rate of return on equity, 3 per cent in real terms.

The analysis's logical core contains *yields on assets/negative yields on liabilities*. Attempts to insert *leverage* into this nub are bound to fail.

2.6 Central banks; monetary policy

Monetary economics is very different from, say, thermodynamics. Monetary theory is mostly implicit: few of its propositions can be rigorously derived from explicit models. And monetary controversies long have been acerbic. The *monetarist* controversy is an example: monetarists insist that control of the monetary base ('high-powered' money) is necessary and sufficient for control of the general price-level; some anti-monetarists say that price-behaviour is uncorrelated with that of the monetary base. Readers of the publications of the St. Louis Federal Reserve Bank and of, say, the recommendations of some Cambridge economists, reported in *The Times* and *The Financial Times* on 21 March 1977, would find it hard to believe that the writers belonged to the same discipline. The absence of explicit modelling has made it impossible to discriminate sharply between competing hypotheses. However, a fairly strong ad hoc consensus, reflected by the loan-conditions imposed by the I.M.F. upon Britain and Italy during 1976–77, seems to have emerged. German and Swiss macro-policies long have been quite monetarist; the French anti-inflation programme of 1976–1977, identified with the Premier, M. Raymond Barre, contains monetary stringency quite exceptional in France.

Several topics in monetary policy will be developed. The analyses admittedly are hard to link up: no field theory spans the material of monetary economics. Indeed the discussion necessarily begins quite abruptly.

Consumers conventionally are perceived in economics as forming expectations of future prices simply by applying weights to past prices. Think of the history of the beef-price. Imagine a prediction of future beef prices based on shuffling up these data in a computer. Even if the procedure were one of decaying exponential weighting, or some other grand-sounding method, it would be fatally flawed: it would make a profound specification error: it would specify the consumer, for example, as being irrational. Rational economic particles would employ the full apparatus of economic theory, together with the best data, subject to cost-efficiency of data collection and processing, in predicting prices. They would not simply shufflle up old price-figures. The quite recent *rational-expectations* literature thus has become important; even in advanced economic theory, transactor-behaviour had been specified to be importantly irrational.

It similarly becomes absurd to specify that the public behaves as if it did not know what the Federal Reserve has said is its policy and as if it did not form conjectures about what the Federal Reserve's policy is and will be. So logic compels us to specify that ongoing monetary policies, together with indications of future policy, *do* affect behaviour directly, not just indirectly: perception of ongoing policy affects behaviour; social experiments inevitably exhibit *feedback*.

But the 'direct' effects just explained belong to the domain of *rational expectations;* they are of a different *genre* from those suggested in the past. Therefore it simply is wrong to say that the public will step up spending plans because they have sold non-monetary assets for cash. In a correct theory, consumer behaviour is constrained by portfolio values, i.e. by wealth, and not by the instantaneous mix of a portfolio each feels free to reconstitute at will. In a correct theory, capital-expenditures reflect expectations of sales/price opportunities relative to costs of capital. True, transactors in the imperfect markets of the real world confront liquidity- as well as wealth-constraints; otherwise-feasible transactions can become barred by inability to encash sufficient assets cheaply and promptly. But this does not undermine the 'Chinese Wall' separating the portfolio-imbalances directly generated by shifts in monetary policy from the 'real' effects mediated by resulting changes in securities and commodities prices.

2.6.1 Indirect transmission

Central-bank monetary operations become translated into changes in the 'real' economy by changes in 'the price of money', to use a crude but evocative term. We shall show that central banks first put the banks into portfolio-disequilibrium, and, indeed, cause general portfolio-imbalance, without significantly affecting net worths. Since each transactor will continue to prefer his initial portfolio at the initial prices of goods and securities, prices must change so that the public will make new portfolio plans, consistent with the revised money-growth path. Of course, the transmission-process is *indirect*.

2.6.2 The work of the chapter: central banks and monetary policy

Treatment of the *logic of monetary policy* will be confined to three major subjects:

(1) The indirect-transmission property.
(2) How deepening of the analysis of effects of inflation-expectations on interest rates has led to a reworking of the 'transmission' analysis.
(3) A frankly keynesian discussion of when a central bank can and when it cannot affect the real rate of interest; there are circumstances that make interest-rate effects of changes in Federal Reserve money-growth policy stand on their heads.

Before exploring the three subjects, we should try to project the reader into *phase space;* economic theory best deals with the *motions* of variables, not with frozen quantums at some moment. So, when dealing with changes in central-bank policy, it is preferable to set up the problem in terms of alternative *paths* for, say, the monetary-base; not for alternative *levels* at some imaginary instant. How would time-paths of prices, outputs, employment(s), etc. be affected if the central bank expanded its credit along vector A instead of vector B?

The ordinary person's difficulty in formulating economic problems dynamically is reflected in high economic theory: the most beautiful economic models are harshly statical. And economists have eschewed general explanations of economic phenomena, once patterned after the field theories of physics, in favour of treatments so specialized to local problems that economics threatens to become unravelled as an integral subject—except for the marvellous Hermann-Hessian Bead Game called 'General Equilibrium Theory'.

(1) INDIRECT TRANSMISSION OF MONETARY POLICY

It is worth attacking this problem from still another direction. Contrast the directness of fiscal policy with the circuitousness of monetary policy. Tax-changes work directly on the public's cash-flow. Higher benefits directly benefit pensioners. Increased government spending transmits itself directly to commodity-demand. True, 'fiscal' effects become diffused in a 'general equilibrium' analysis encompassing chains of derivative effects. 'Crowding out' supplies an example. The ultimate effect of increased public spending on demand-for-all-goods may be *nil:* the higher public sector borrowing requirement may push up interest rates so that private-sector spending is depressed pound-for-pound with the increase in public spending.

Considering open-market operations by central banks, interest rates and portfolio (im)balance will be directly affected. And since continuing effects on interest rates will flow from consequences of portfolio imbalance, we move straight on to *open-market operations and portfolio imbalance.*

Federal Reserve open-market operations are conducted in Government securities markets, usually for near maturities. So, putting aside *repurchase agreements,* it might seem that sellers of securities purchased by the Federal Reserve will have been induced to want to reduce their holdings; even this attractive inference is specious, although the companion inference, that they will acquire excess demand-deposits, is sustained.

Now probe into the position of a specialist—the usage is loosely based on share-trading—in a Government security used in open-market operations. His 'book' will display data that can build up what may seem to be, but which are not, supply and demand schedules for the security. Perhaps, just before the opening, there are buying orders for

4,000 units at a price of 98 and selling orders for 5,000 or more units at a price of 98 or more. Surely the security will not be opened at 98. *Now* word comes from Liberty Street, from the Federal Reserve Bank of New York: the open-market operator will buy 1,000 units at 98 or less. The security *will* open at 98. Five-thousand units will be traded; an open-market purchase of 1,000 units will be consummated.

A specialist on an open-market security is not omniscient, like the *crieur* in a facet of the Bead Game: he knows little about the demand configurations of the holders of the vast majority of the stock; they will have given him no indications at all. Perhaps the price prevailing at yesterday's close, 97·875, equilibrated yesterday's market.[2] And 1,000 units represents only a tiny fraction of the stock in question: 97·875 may still equilibrate the market; an omniscient *crieur* might arrive at 97·875 too.

The imbalance generated by an open-market transaction at 98 may be general: if Security X were reported at 98, the prices of the many securities substitutional or complementary with X no longer would clear their markets.

What if the price of X settled back at 97·875? The open-market purchase still would cause two disturbances. One will result from the injection of demand deposits into the system. These demand deposits will unbalance portfolios: holders will want to dispose of them. The clearing banks also will be out of equilibrium: they will have excess reserves of $98,000, less the reserves required to support $98,000 in additional deposits.

The non-banking public will have excess demands for all sorts of securities reflecting the excess supply of demand deposits. And the clearing banks will want to absorb their excess liquidity. Securities markets will be affected but, since there will have been no significant effects on wealth,[3] there will be almost no incentive to spend cash on 'real' goods. Whatever are the effects of portfolio imbalance, they surely are indirect.

(2) INFLATION EXPECTATIONS, ETC.

Until quite recently, most writers simply would say that the pressures, due to portfolio imbalances, created by open-market purchases would cause lower interest rates. Now almost all writers are much more guarded; certain conjectures of Irving Fisher have been revived.

In physical sciences the behaviour of the particles under study is independent of the theories about them. This need not be true in economics; *inflation expectations and interest rates* are a prime example. Economists' theories may lead to a consensus forecast that accelerating money-growth will induce a higher inflation-rate: lenders and borrowers will, *as a result,* expect the purchasing power of a given stream of interest-payments to deteriorate. Consequent behavioural adaptations are studied in Section 2.8.

2.7 Rational expectations

An economic nexus contains a *conjectural symbiosus* between policy makers and the members of the economy. A rational public with access, however indirect, to information available to the authorities will 'discount' official actions. Such a public will absorb as data complete descriptions of 'conditional' official action-plans as well as 'resultant' official actions, say in the fields of tax-rates or levels of public spending. The public will know how official response is formed; the officials will know that the public knows. . . .

Consider rational public response to a dynamic, 'unstabilized' economic process.

Plans of households and firms will be made relative to well-defined economic models subject to random disturbance. Assume that these random disturbances have nil expected values and are symmetrical.

Plans are formed. The most important plans, especially those concerning purchase of consumers' and producers' durable goods, will be little affected by the random disturbance process. This implies that disturbances will die away quickly so that cumulative destabilizing processes are highly unlikely.

Now assume that the government wants to reduce the amplitude of the economy's randomly impelled oscillation. Can it do so? Perhaps not if the government behaves predictably.

First analyse the problem 'traditionally'. Assume that random disturbances $u_1, u_2, \ldots, u_n$ 'bombard' the economy during periods $(t =)$ 1, 2, $\ldots, n$. These disturbances have known consequences—whether or not the members of the economy are fully informed and rational—so that χ_{14} and χ_{36} measure the effects of u_1 and u_3 at $t = 4$ and $t = 6$. It is reasonable to assume that official response to u will be lagged so that ε_{23} measures official response to u_2 at $t = 3$—the lag here being one period. And λ_{23} measures the effect of ε_{12} at $t = 3$. So the combined effect at $t = 3$ of random disturbance *cum* official 'stabilizing' response would be

$$\chi_{13} + \chi_{23} + u_3 + \lambda_{23} + \varepsilon_{23}$$

and λ_{23} (reflecting ε_{12}) and ε_{23} would, in a stabilizing regime, be calculated to offset χ_{13} and χ_{23}, at least if the disturbance process were not inherently oscillatory, let alone undamped. Ideally, in a stabilizing regime, the net disturbance effect at $t = 3$ would be u_3. And, of course, the disturbance effects, thus limited to $u_1, u_2, \ldots u_n$, would be serially uncorrelated: for example, the expected covariance of u_t and u_{t-1} would be zero.

Taking up a *laissez-faire* regime and inserting *rational expectations* into the analysis, the disturbance effect at $t = 3$ would be $\chi_{13} + \chi_{23} + u_3$. *But,* in certain circumstances under rational expectations,

$$\chi_{13} + \chi_{23} = 0$$

If price-bevahiour were being modelled, an economy rationally employing available information would act in ways barring serial correlation of disturbances. χ_{13} and χ_{23} are predictable from data accumulated before $t = 3$; this predictability would induce profit-taking until arbitrage enforced serial non-correlation so that

$$\chi_{13} + \chi_{23} = 0(!)$$

Rational-expectations theory implies much about securities and commodity-market behaviour. Its impact upon economic-stabilization theory depends on how predictability and profitability deploy about the unemployment rate and housing starts as well as price behaviour: can arbitrageurs profit from serial correlation in the unemployment rate (?); would such arbitrage affect that rate?

Assume that the deviation of the unemployment rate from its *natural level* is a function of the difference between the actual change in the price level, p, and the expected change, p^e. Under rational expectations, the series $(p - p^e)_t$ will be serially uncorrelated. Next assume that price-change is in a 1:1 relationship to the growth-rate of money-supply, m. Then, where the unemployment rate is U and the 'natural' value of U is suppressed,

$$U = f(p - p^e) = f(m - m^e).$$

Alternatively, if the deviation of U from its natural value, u, were a function of $(p - p^e)$, so that $u = f(p - p^e)$, the unemployment rate, U, would indirectly be in a simple monotonic relationship with $(m - m^e)$.

Unemployment, even in the short run would be affected only by unpredictable movements in money-growth. The authorities would have to turn to wild play to influence the unemployment rate; predictably-behaving authorities would be impotent.

2.7.1 Sources of perturbation

The public sector supplies some of the more-interesting sources of perturbation. Money supply may surge above its normal growth rate. Tax collections briefly may shoot up. A rational economy would not *project* such events so long as the perturbations were perceived to be randomly accidental.

Amplifying the money-supply vignette, the public, knowing that money-growth soon would diminish, regaining its longer-run norm, would not be misled. True, very-short interest rates might fall. But pressures on prices based on false inflation-expectations would be cancelled by arbitrageurs.

2.7.2 Informal reflections on rational expectations and stabilization policy

If economic actors are rational and well informed, they will need no guidance in order to get back on track after a random perturbation: it would make no sense for government expenditure to lurch backwards because unexpected drought abroad may have increased grain exports for example. Agreed, some relative-price adjustments might then be necessary; there might be a blip on the curve tracking the general price level. But the mechanical and stochastic problems besetting the timing of the government's cumbrous 'stabilizing' response would be more likely to increase than decrease the economy's turbulence.

The more rational and fully informed are the particles of an economy, the more promptly can it absorb shocks; wave-like motions will be suppressed. So, especially in view of characteristic sluggishness in government response (always 'politically' conditioned), the more rational is a fully-informed economy, the more likely will be 'stabilizing' authorities to agitate a self-adjusting process.

A government may be cognizant of the logic of rational expectations and anxious to preserve its sense of power of intervention. Under strong rational-expectations stipulations, it would have to withhold information from and deceive the public; at the least it would have to behave erratically. Indeed the public might eke out the official strategy relative to the contingencies supplied by nature. The government then could preserve its 'freedom of action' only by transforming its action-path into a random variable!

2.8 Interest rates and inflation expectations

Interest rates may rise because they have fallen!

Interest rates may be pushed down by pressure from open-market purchases; the banks' excess liquidity will propel monetary expansion as banks purchase more securities, partly through fresh lending.

The slide in interest rates will signal that monetary expansion is speeding up. If inflation-expectations thus are triggered, causing lenders to demand higher nominal yields and impelling borrowers to take down more funds at implicitly lower real rates of interest, lower interest rates *will* cause higher ones.

2.8.1 Response to higher expected inflation

Ex ante reasoning suggests many responses, varying in strength and even in direction.

The borrowers' side is quite clear-cut. If investment projects' expected real returns are invariant against inflation-expectations, it becomes attractive to float more projects, to borrow more at given nominal interest rates, pushing up interest rates.

The lender's side is less straightforward. Households often save more when inflation-expectations are strong: the real value of existing money-fixed savings is expected to erode: nest-eggs must be bolstered. True, households own other sorts of claims: real estate, consumer durables, equities, etc. Still these alternatives are flawed as savings media. Real-estate-investment values collapsed in 1974–1975; consumer durables either are illiquid or unstable in price; equity investment is risky and share-prices have lagged inflation for some time.

Financial institutions are less supple even than households in implementing inflation-expectations. Indeed to the considerable extent that their liabilities are money-fixed (cf. life-insurance companies) they have no reason to be 'supple'.

Legal and customary prudential constraints impose limits on institutional investment in equities or real estate. (Of course, building societies are overwhelmingly invested in real estate; they are strongly inhibited in other directions.) And surely banks and insurance companies do not directly acquire durable goods as inflation-hedges.

2.9 Remarks on equity-values

Share prices are heavily affected by interest rates and inflation-expectations and so are highly sensitive to central-bank actions and anticipations of central-bank actions.

Dividends are discounted just like other long-lived income streams. In a world of perfectly-balanced inflation of nominal values, earnings and dividends of all companies would experience the same inflation-rate; shares would sell at unchanged multiples of dividends. Thus assume that, 'pre-inflation', Company A paid an annual dividend of $1, discounted at 5 per cent; A shares were priced at $20. Now assume a balanced 7 per cent inflation. The A-dividend will grow at 7 per cent and be discounted at 12 per cent:

$$P_A \cong \int^{\infty} e^{.07} / \int^{\infty} e^{.12} \cong \int^{\infty} e^{-.05} \cong 20$$

Or simply assume that the real interest rate stays at 5 per cent and the real dividend at $1. The share-price must be $20 for the real yield to be 5 per cent.

It might seem that the real value of the share is depreciating. No! The dividend will increase at 7 per cent per annum and the multiple will rest at 20: the nominal share-price will increase at 7 per cent p.a. from its initial price of $20; its real value will be constant.

Inflation is not balanced in the real world. Thus, if A's dividend were expected to grow at 2 per cent, its share-price would plummet to 10. In general, the additional uncertainties of the 'inflation lottery' make share-prices more volatile and equity investment less liquid; sustained inflation, sustained unbalanced inflation in the real world, is a drag on the Market.

Chapter 6, *Share Prices,* deepens the analysis of *autocorrelation of residuals:* if the well-established tendency of an efficient share market to eliminate correlation of errors in the predictions of its underlying model is transferable to macro-economic stabilization theory, traditional 'stabilization' policies can be destabilizing.

(3) CENTRAL BANKS AND REAL RATES OF INTEREST
2.10 Crowding Out

Before Keynes, the conventional wisdom, embodied in the British 'Treasury View', was that increased public spending would not increase national income: fresh public spending would *crowd out* that much private spending. The volume of savings, i.e. resources available to absorb non-consumption expenditure, was thought to be fixed. Keynes's theory, now dominant, is that the volume of savings is not fixed and that, indeed, levels of savings and national income are determined by *autonomous expenditure.*

Autonomous crumbles on reflection. When is human action not reaction to *something?* To call something autonomous is to avoid asking why it does what it does. And, if the logic of 'autonomousness' is taken into the limit, the economy pivots on earthquakes, droughts, floods and other forces of nature.

In keynesian economics a variable excluded from the domain of explication, an autonomous variable, is preeminent; it helps drive the system.

A *bathtub* analogue displays the role of autonomous investment in keynesian theory. The *mise en scène* follows.

Water leaks out of the tub at a rate rigidly linked to the level of water in the tub. If the leakage-coefficient is $0 \cdot 10$ and if the water-level is 100, 10 units per period will leak out. The analogous economic process concerns savings leaks from the circular flow of income; *the marginal propensity to save,* taken to be equal to the average propensity, would be $0 \cdot 10$.

The rate of inflow of water into the tub, A, is autonomous. The level of water, Y, will be rising when

$$A > sY$$

and falling when

$$A < sY$$

For $Y = \bar{Y}$, for the water-level to be in equilibrium,

$$A = sY$$

So

$$\Delta \bar{Y} = (1/s)\, \Delta A$$

Thus the *multiplier*.

Private investment expenditure, together with public spending, were specified to be autonomous in earlier keynesian literature. This no longer is acceptable. In ways importantly influenced by Keynes, much public spending is responsive to fluctuations in economic-growth rates. And spending that is not obviously *endogenous* often looks endogenous under subtle scrutiny: increases in defence spending are more palatable politically when unemployment is high; almost all private-sector capital-expenditures reflect anticipations necessarily influenced by experience (!).

Two sketchy remarks may be made in this connection.

(1) Private-sector capital expenditures tend to be pro-cyclical, albeit lagged; much stabilization policy has concerned official efforts to combat this pro-cyclicality.

(2) Some capital expenditures, e.g. those related to technological breakthrough or profound changes in consumer attitudes, along lines developed by Joseph Schumpeter, are importantly autonomously based.

2.10.1 Interpolations

(1) *Transfer payments* must be distinguished from public-sector demands for goods and services. Taxes are negative transfer payments; taxation reduces private demand for goods to some extent, creating 'room' for other activities. Although the government does not demand goods when it pays subsidies, subsidies increase private demand to some extent, restricting space available for other activities. Transfer payments might lead up to some private-sector spending crowding out other private-sector spending but do not cause public- to crowd out private-spending.

(2) Under Keynes's theory, there need not be 1:1 substitution in favour of transfer-payment fuelled private spending and against other private spending. If tax rates are increased or decreased, national income will fall or rise.

(3) If the public sector were to finance increased expenditure by raising taxes in full-employment conditions, the upshot would *not* be called crowding out. *Crowding out* concerns effects of increased public-sector budget-deficits brought about by higher public spending; it concerns the possibility that, then, private spending would get crowded out

although tax provisions stood the same.

2.10.2 Completion of the crowding-out discussion

The affirmative crowding-out proposition, asserted by the British Treasury of yore and the *Wall Street Journal* always, is

> Private spending will decrease dollar for dollar with the increase in public spending; private debt-issues will be withdrawn from the market as borrowers become discouraged by higher interest rates.

The informed (by Keynes) proposition is

> Private spending will decrease dollar for dollar with increased debt-financed public spending if and only if (iff) the economy is at full employment; the volume of savings cannot otherwise be taken as fixed.

The 'informed' proposition has got a corollary that, in practice, much reduces the distance between the affirmative and 'informed' positions.

> *COROLLARY* Substantial unemployment among teenagers and unskilled married women cannot push back binding constraints imposed by full employment of skilled workers and machine-capacities. The macroscopic unemployment statistic can be misleading, even useless. Effectively-full employment can occur when the macroscopic unemployment is 7 or 8 per cent.

It remains to defend the *informed proposition*. Analysis of the *natural rate of interest* will be based on congruent reasoning.

Assume that all productive capacities are less than fully employed. Increased debt-financed public spending will be self-financing in the sense that it will generate, through a multiplier effect, savings equal to itself; the savings rate in the new equilibrium will be higher by precisely the amount, reckoned as a flow, by which the investment tap has been turned up. In this, *keynesian,* case increased public spending generates its own savings and thus is self-financing. The benignity of the huge, controversial American federal deficits of fiscal 1975 and 1976 becomes explained.

The affirmative proposition is a special case of the 'informed' proposition: real income may not be responsive to a public-spending impulse: take the 'full employment' case. Then increased public spending cannot finance itself. (Higher interest rates, brought about by pressures of increased public issues on money markets, may induce higher savings rates; *both* propositions should be qualified accordingly.)

2.10.3 *Afterword on crowding out: the role of the central bank; politics*

Public spending might increase when there is 'generalized' excess capacity. Then the central bank properly could expand the monetary base enough to enable money-supply to increase to meet additional demand for money, induced by higher national product.

If the public-sector deficit is expanded in a strictly fully-employed economy, the central bank properly would not *monetize* new public debt. Then an accelerating monetary base would impart a fillip to interest rates as inflationary expectations became ignited. Then crowding out would become overshadowed by a collapse of private investment, especially if inflation prospects looked likely to produce political incoherence.

Central-bank prudence in the 'strict full employment' case would outrage most politicians and disconcert many economists. Would the compound event, *central-bank prudence/political inflammation,* boost or depress the stock market? Perhaps the Market would admire the Bank. They admire profit more; they are likely to fear a political tempest more than they would draw inspiration from the courage of the Bank. Thus one notes how British share prices as late as July 1977 moved sympathetically with the fortunes of the Labour Government, importantly because of the City's fears of confrontation between a Thatcher (Tory) Government and the unions. Yet hardly a man in the City doubted that Mrs Thatcher was intellectually correct; very few of these Labour supporters were other than anti-Socialist.

'Watergate' began in August 1971. President Nixon, applauded by Wall Street, reversed his prudent economic policy and imposed wage/price controls. This provided to be a prelude to rapid monetary expansion in 1972; President Nixon was anxious to reverse his then hapless position in the impending 1972 election; the Federal Reserve may have connived with him. Wall Street was elated.

The Dow Jones Industrial Average surpassed 1,000 in Autumn 1973, despite continuing zigzags in an Administration policy heavily responsive to the unfolding Watergate scandal. Then there was the brutal 1974–75 recession, exacerbated by the Government's erratic behaviour. The Dow almost fell below 500 during 1974.

2.11 Full employment

Keynes argued that, normally, an advanced economy's resources would not be fully employed save for substantial public-sector spending. *Full employment* concerns buildings, machines, land, etc., and *people;* it, and its concomitant *rate of unemployment concept,* are hard to define.

Think of a gas whose molecules are in one of two states: green or red; employed or umemployed. The proportion of red molecules measures the unemployment-rate.

Another measurement concerns *the average duration of an unemployment-experience*. The proportion of molecules in a red state may rise and the average duration of a red state may fall; the unemployment-rate may rise and the average-duration of an unemployment-experience may fall. If the average duration of a red state became very short, the red/red+green ratio would become socially unimportant.

Another model supplies an analogue to the *vacancy rate*. And analogues to the unemployment rate, the average duration of unemployment, the vacancy rate, the quit rate and the hiring rate all are wanted.

In the second model, the state variable is adhesion/non-adhesion. In it colour is an invariant property: worker-molecules are orange; employer-molecules are blue. Neither worker- nor employer-molecules adhere to each other. Adhesion of a worker-molecule to an employer-molecule comprises an employment-relationship. There are multiple adhesions to employers. Some workers will divide themselves and adhere to a number of employers. The vacancy-rate is measured by the proportion of unrequited blue adhesion-requests to actual adhesions. The unemployment rate is the proportion of celibate orange molecules to the total of orange molecules. The quit rate is the proportion of orange particles peeling away from blue molecules over one year to the average number of adhesions during the year, just as the proportion borne by new adhesions to that number gives the annual hiring-rate.

Operating the second model, in scenario A the molecules move sluggishly: celibate molecules meander lackadaisically, searching for partners. In scenario B the molecules move in quick time: quit- and vacancy-rates are high. 'B''s unemployment-rate will depend upon the *parameters* controlling *search*.

If orange molecules, having broken liaisons with blue molecules, receive generous unemployment benefits, they will, however rapid their movements, be loath to re-engage. If there were no unemployment benefits, disengaged orange molecules would be undiscriminating about 'remarriage'.

Some of the parameters of a physical counterpart to the unemployment model could not be manipulated; these are general environmental properties. Other parameters would be *controls*: the experimenter could affect the gases by changing air pressure, temperature, rotational motion of the container, etc.

In the unemployment model, some 'general environmental' properties would be demographic: proportions of women, youths and pensioners in the labour-force, etc. Others would be 'economic', e.g., the growth-rate of the industrial sector and accumulated household savings. Controls would include the terms of unemployment-benefit, job-search assistance, minimum-wage legislation, etc.

It is hard to define *involuntary unemployment*. Is a man who refuses a job-offer in order to continue his search for a better job involuntarily unemployed? It would be futile to try to supply an answer. Rather we shall deal with unemployment *pur et simple*.

Attitudes towards unemployment will depend upon *who* is unemployed. The fact that so much American unemployment recently has been concentrated among young blacks has made the problem politically less exigent, especially since this unemployment is concentrated in urban centres that blindly vote Democratic. Nor would one expect the South African Government to be mesmerized by moderate increases in black unemployment. Nor would unemployment anywhere among housewives seeking outside work or among their children excite concern as much as would unemployment among their husbands, the traditional breadwinners.

If indeed unemployment is responsive to policy, one must study *trade-offs*: resource-mobility demands some unemployment; attempts to reduce unemployment can accelerate inflation. One's attitudes towards these trade-offs will depend upon the extent to which the pain of unemployment characteristically is assuaged by compensation, on its average duration, etc.

The most celebrated unemployment trade-off probably concerns *unemployment and inflation*.

It has been believed, since the war, until recently, that more-rapid monetary expansion almost always would lower the unemployment rate, albeit perhaps increasing inflation. The result became formulated in a phrase, the 'Phillips Curve'.

2.11.1 The Phillips curve

The argument yielding the Phillips Curve is fatally flawed. It is based upon the public being *irrational*.

Why should companies offer more jobs because of monetary expansion?

Perhaps accelerated monetary expansion will stimulate securities markets, including those for consumer credit, in ways we have explained. Easier credit will stimulate demand for goods. Profit margins will increase: plants will be operated nearer to minimum-unit-cost output-levels; prices will rise relatively to wages since wage bargains tend to be 'sticky'. The second facet implies that real-wages either will fall or that their growth will slip below 'trend'. Both facets imply that more labour will be hired or that employment-growth will rise above 'trend'.

Was the unemployment-rate initially at its natural level? If it were above its natural level, the analysis can be diverted into the stream of keynesian income theory. So we shall assume that, initially, the unemployment-rate was at its natural level. *Then* the problem becomes,

Is the natural-rate *stable?* Will the unemployment-rate return to its natural level if it is displaced from it?

The equilibrium containing the natural rate of unemployment will be stable if the members of the economy are rational. Then the wage-rate corresponding to the natural rate of unemployment will be defined in *real* terms, crudely, a certain value of the ratio w/p.

Stability effectively requires merely that, if p were for a time to increase more rapidly than w, w, the money-wage unit, subsequently would run ahead of p, restoring the equilibrium value of w/p. The 'unnaturally' tight labour markets associated with lower-than-natural rates of unemployment will assure that wage rates *do* surge ahead.

There should be *no* trade-off between inflation, based on more-rapid expansion of the money-supply, and unemployment.

2.11.2 Fiscal policy à outrance

Governments *can* achieve very low unemployment rates. Massive public-sector spending, including made-work projects, surely can press down unemployment-rates to near-zero levels. Hitler proved that.

Fiscal policy *à outrance* and its concomitantly bloated public sector do confront a decisive barrier:[4] some productive resources will be scarce. (Such a government would not let 'inadequate' money-supply impede its programme—it would print uninhibitedly.) The barrier thrown up by scarce-resource limitations would, in such a regime, have at least two crucial consequences. First, persistent excess demand for scarce resources would cause their prices persistently to rise. Secondly, the stagnant or declining output of the private sector under fiscal policy *à outrance* would have to be shared out more and more stringently as public-sector demand became more pressing.

Usually a government carrying out so bloated a fiscal policy will be *dirigiste*. As the 'stagflationary' consequences of their policy unfold, they will impose price controls *suppressing* underlying inflation. *Suppressed inflation* leads to shortages, queues and quality deterioration in lieu of visible price increases. Suppressed inflation is apt to be more harmful than open inflation: it distorts relative prices. The price controls and incomes policies characterizing a regime of suppressed inflation usually flow from a diagnosis of *cost-push* inflation.

Obviously the revenues of suppliers are costs to buyers; prices received by suppliers are paid by customers. In the real world, positive demand-shifts usually lead first to inventory (stock) run-down, following a sequence flowing upstsream from final demand towards raw-material supply. Upstream companies, as they increase their demands for raw materials, will experience cost-increases. So their *supply prices* will rise. Supply-price increases, beginning upstsream, will transmit themselves downstream. Higher costs will become transformed into higher prices, comprising higher costs further downstream. Excess-demand-based inflation thus acquires the look of cost-push.

2.11.3 Remarks on incomes policy

Incomes policies contain wage controls, accompanied by 'dividend restraint' and price controls. Wage suppression becomes substantially offset by wage drift: job classifications, for example, get more liberal: Class B jobs become Class A jobs.

The highly visible negotiations between trade unions and major companies attract much notice. One reason why it often seems that inflation is triggered by these and other wage-demands is that unionized wage-bargains in particular, and wage-bargains generally, are 'sticky': there are longer lags in wage- than in price-response to underlying inflationary pressure. The process governing increasing supply prices of workers tends to be erratic and brusque. So, especially if the inflation has been suppressed, so that the ways in which worker-income has lagged are less visible, it becomes easy, albeit improper, to blame inflation on workers and their unions.

A quite-separate matter concerns some unions, usually in the public sector, able to extract a high price for their services because these services, taken *en bloc* are vital; think of electricity. The effect of exactions of this sort is like that of the massive increase in the oil-price *circa* late 1973/1974. There are redistributive effects: union members become wealthier at the expense of the rest of the economy. To the extent that the (negative) impact on profits is substantial, economic growth may slow down. But such exactions are no more *inflationary* than once-over increases in excise taxes. And, like such tax-increases, once-over increases in price-levels are followed by a continuing drag on aggregate demand. *Inflation concerns rising, not higher, prices.*

The commonest argument for incomes policy is *post hoc, propter hoc*. It is said that, if incomes rise less rapidly, so will prices. But the social accounting identities imply this: national income and gross domestic product are definitionally linked. The 'argument' really says that inflation is *caused* by higher prices! The fallacy is as pervasive, in a number of directions, as it is perverse.

2.11.4 Disguised unemployment

A society may fail to sustain a growing working population at rising per capita income. Then it might pump up public-sector employment, sharing out misery, perhaps in ways clogging capital-expansion.

In the 1930s there was little reason, in advanced countries, to worry about increased public spending: it was low to start with; the proposals were picayune by present standards. Substantial excess capacity was common; pump priming was plausible. Theoretical developments, due to Keynes, made it plausible to expect increased public spending to generate offsetting real savings. Theoretical developments, due to Harrod, made it plausible to expect resulting increases in demands for produced goods to stimulate investment expenditures (thus *the accelerator*).

In the 1970s, in country after country, public sectors have been sucking in growing quantities of outputs capable of satisfying economic wants and absorbing resources that otherwise would augment capital-goods production. It is a sad spectacle of the times. Less-developed countries, starved for capital, practise a fiscality recommended by Keynes to advanced, wealthy countries, however much played out.

2.11.5 *More on the natural rate of unemployment*

If all, or too much, of the labour force always were to find employment, overall demand would have to be *so* strong that there would be persistent excess demand for many resources, including many types of labour. The complementary crowding-out concept, suggesting that hyperactive public spending would, by absorbing many scarce resources with attendant consequences for interest rates, suppress private investment, buttresses the conjecture. Expansion of non-human capacities would stall; over-stimulated demand would collide with depressed supply-growth. Thus *stagflation*.

The natural-rate-of-unemployment concept is but a loose imitation of an older idea. There long has bounced about in economics the notion of some kind of *natural rate of interest*.

2.12 The natural-rate-of-interest idea

We develop a natural-rate-of-interest idea attributable to Keynes.

When can central-bank action affect the real rate of interest?

The central bank can drive down the real rate of interest if it lies above the natural rate, but not otherwise. Fiscal, but not monetary, actions can drive up the real rate of interest (cf. crowding-out).

It is theoretically possible that:

For an economy's private sector to attain an expansion-path consistent with full employment, the long-term rate of interest would have to be lower than permitted by the *liquidity preference* of the public. The public might refuse to hold longer-term securities yielding so little. Thus the *liquidity trap*.

The *real rate of interest* is a nebulous idea: each expects, uncertainly, different price-behaviour. This thicket can be avoided by rephrasing the answer to the query, 'when can central-bank action affect the real rate of interest?'

Assume that inflation-expectations stay the same. Then the central bank can drive down 'the' observed, i.e. nominal or objective, interest-rate so long as it lies above the nominal rate of interest consistent with full employment. Not otherwise.

Tightening up the revised answer, monetary expansion may speed up; interest rates may begin to fall. If there is a fringe of idle resources, lower interest rates will stick: injection of extra liquidity into the system then would satisfy demands for extra cash associated with accelerated economic activity; incremental investment would be financed by incremental savings incident to higher national income. If there is no fringe of idle resources, lower interest rates will not stick; nor will rational inflation-expectations stay the same. If there is no fringe of idle resources, attempts to take advantage of lower interest rates, and perhaps higher share prices, simply will push up price-inflation; higher inflation will absorb the fresh liquidity and provoke higher observed (nominal) interest rates.

2.13 Concluding observations

Central banks do not supply resources that can be put to work to increase real national product; they simply affect states of liquidity and credit-market conditions. So, if an economy verges upon full employment and if its real growth-rate is to increase, savings- and investment-propensities must be stimulated. If an economy is meaningfully below full employment, stimulation of its investment-propensity, perhaps through cheaper money, can initiate a real-growth process that is self-financing and hence self-sustaining. Then, increased real income will generate increased savings financing an augmented investment stream.

It might seem that the 'real' economy becomes invariant against central-bank action once the Bank has expanded the reserve-base at least as rapidly as liquidity-preference requires; that, once enough liquidity has been supplied to validate the natural rate of interest, the real economy is independent of the path of price inflation or expected inflation. Such is not the case.

Inflation and the real economy are in fact linked. Thus share prices fall with expectations of higher inflation importantly because inflations are not uniform; one is reminded how in physics propositions based on uniform motion can give way to ones associated with accelerated and other non-uniform motions.

The most erratic motions contemplated in economic policy are those of politicians. The responses of politicians to the inflations they have made have come to be the worst consequences of inflation. Inefficiencies in resource allocation, clogs to growth and adverse effects on profits, induced by incomes policies, price controls, dividend restraints, etc., are to be expected when higher inflation is expected.

Perhaps the most interesting new direction explored in Chapter 2 concerns deeper study of *expectations*. It now is understood that economics must be concerned with the behaviour of intelligent animals.

3 Money Supply Control in the U.S.

Preliminary discussion

It also is true in London, Paris, Frankfurt, Milan, Zurich. The Federal Reserve's influence on the American economy radiates out from the New York money market. There is much in monetary economics, so rooted in institutional arrangements, akin to Maitland's dictum that substantive law is secreted in the interstices of procedure. And physical analogies are correspondingly dubious: there is no close correspondence in monetary economics with say wave-like or corpuscular-like theories of emanation; the money market's reactions to Federal Reserve actions are not mathematically well defined. For one thing, the Federal Reserve never clearly etches out its programme of action. Nor is it clear that the Board ever has a *completely* worked out programme: one studies the Board in the way that one studies other organisms uncertainly responding in broadly optimizing ways to phenomena of uncertain purport and origin.

An open-market sale may be intended to make the Market less liquid. Or it may be offsetting 'operational' factors such as large transfers of U.S. Government deposits from Federal-Reserve to clearing banks. The sale may be part of a strategy for draining reserves from the banking system; the sale may be part of a neutral strategy and may offset seasonally technical forces supplying reserves to the banks; the sale may be part of a neutral strategy and may offset a chance event supplying reserves to the banks. The truth may never be known.

The Market will respond to 'open-market events' relative to its memory. And its response will be jagged for at least three reasons. The Market cannot be *sure* about Federal Reserve intentions, let alone Federal Reserve reaction to disappointment or surprise. No trader in the Market can be sure about how other traders are going to respond. The track of the economy, the stimulus to Federal Reserve action (relative to FR objectives), cannot be precisely ascertained. The first and second reasons for 'jagged' Market response to perceived 'open market' events are imbedded in the *social* properties of economic studies: as was so much stressed in Chapter 2, in the modern theory of economic policy,

49

impulses transmitted by policy-makers towards the economy do not simply, unidirectionally work their way through the economy; instead the sensient, intelligent beings comprising the economy modify their behaviour, relative to their own objectives, in accordance with their perception of the official reaction function, requiring a revision of policy if indeed such response was not officially anticipated. *Feedback* is of the essence; a sort of equilibrium can emerge only if the equivalent of a *saddle-point* in game-theory is achieved so that no party can improve its pay-off relative to the strategy being employed by any other party. Nor should the elements of the economy be regarded as inorganic lumps of material in their interaction with each other. And, since their number is so large, one anticipates that a correct theory of the interaction of the particles comprising the economy would stress competition rather than cooperation. One thinks of what I have called *the burden of the money supply*[1]. If, for example, it is widely anticipated that money-growth is going to accelerate, there will be a positive pay-off to those able to reduce their money-balances before general attempts at such reduction set in . . . . The third reason for 'jagged' response stresses that, in social science, errors of observation tend to be larger than in physical science, just as 'social' theories tend to be much looser than 'physical' theories so that errors in social equations tend to be greater. Indeed there is a loose and uncertain relationship in economic theory between the matter of the theory and that which can be observed.

Behavioural properties of financial markets

Seen up close, day by day, Markets seem neurasthenic and rumour-prone in a world in which data inputs are transformed into outputs subject to random perturbations *so* massive compared to those of physical systems. Yet it seems exceptionally hard to take advantage of them, however inadequate the performance of financial markets; it seems very hard to 'beat' them. Why?

In a useful scientific methodology, hypotheses are not inherently true or false, good or bad. One chooses between hypotheses, in the simplest case, between null and alternative hypotheses.

Tests based on financial data have overwhelmingly supported null hypotheses (cf. Chapter 6). Experiments persistently lead to *rejection* of hypotheses that time-series of price-changes of securities are usefully correlated. So experiments persistently lead to *acceptance* of the hypothesis that one's best guide for a market-strategy is the assumption that one cannot expect to be able to predict how securities prices will change. Experimentation encourages one to select securities portfolios in the way one selects one's insurance-policy portfolio. One does not buy fire insurance because one expects one's house to burn down. Instead, insurance rationally is bought relative to analysis of contingency-effects, relative to conditional probability distributions. Similarly, portfolio-managers properly can take into account historical data-behaviour: expected variance of the value of some initial portfolio might be reduced by a reshuffle so that significant portions of the portfolio are—based on historic performance—negatively covariant with each other; I do not know if the price of Share S is going to go up or down tomorrow; I expect that, if the price of S goes up (down), that of V will go down (up) correspondingly. (Again cf. Chapter 6 where the upshot is perhaps expressed more agnostically.)

Some rejected alternative hypotheses would explain the data 'technically'. These hypotheses assert that a security's price-data form patterns so that, when a pattern is far enough advanced to permit the 'technician' to 'anticipate how it will complete itself, a profitable long or short position can be taken in the security. Of course, the null hypothesis denies that such speculation can be expected to be profitable.

Other alternative hypotheses are 'fundamentally' based. Fundamentalist hypotheses are rooted in formulas of natural security values, due account being taken of the discount rates determining the general cost of capital and the extent to which necessarily historical performance-data might be irrelevant to future performance. On the whole, such hypotheses have been 'defeated' by null hypotheses rooted in *random* selection; in no case has a fundamentalist hypothesis proved itself superior to the null at a high level of significance.

The implications of what has been (to Wall Street) the shocking 'combat-ineffectiveness' of fundamentalist hypotheses are not at all crystal clear (again cf. Chapter 6). True, one pragmatic response has encouraged 'indexed' investment, i.e. portfolio-balance imitating the weighting of say the Standard & Poor '500'. An interesting, if perhaps extreme, response has been the *efficient market hypothesis*.

Some reluctantly have accepted that known fundamentalist principles of investment strategy indeed look 'combat-ineffective'. (Why reluctantly? Persons who enjoy speculating like to think that there is reason in their rhymes.) Such persons, surely if exercising fiducial responsibility, would, at the least, be less inclined to take vulnerable positions based on strategic theory. Others have gone *much* farther.

The efficient-market hypothesis holds that *no* investment strategy can be expected to lead to a higher total return than one obtainable from random selection because the Market acts as if it were as well informed as one can be well informed and then optimally processes this information according to correct economic theory. Obviously, such a Market would be unbeatable.

Those holding the efficient-market hypothesis readily admit that securities or commodities prices will fluctuate. Supporters of the hypothesis go on to say that the change from say yesterday to today in the price of security or commodity X has two components. One component will have been expected: if the Market, relative to all data at hand yesterday, expected to assign a multiple (price/earnings ratio) of 15 to X's annualized earnings-rate as of today, and if it assigned the same multiple to yesterday's annualized earnings, the same as those expected for today, then the Market expected to assign the same price to X today as yesterday.[2] The second component results from information developing today that could not have been anticipated yesterday. One cannot expect to profit from actions taken today relative to tomorrow's unknown developments.

Chapter 6 will deepen and extend these remarks. It suffices here to note how Federal Reserve strategy would interact with efficient markets. Chapter 2 has elaborately developed the ways in which central-bank activity affects, however transitorily, various interest rates and the extent to which liquidity comes to be considered excessive or inadequate. Central-bank actions can be expected to affect stock- and other markets from day to day. And, if markets are efficient, 'The Market' will know as much as can be known about how the central bank will react to contingent circumstances. So, to the extent that factors external to the central bank and the Market were quiescent (in life they never are quiescent), central-bank action would be discounted by the Market; 'Federal Reserve watching' could not be profitable. Eruptions of external factors could not be a source of profit either. One cannot anticipate the unknowable. The consequences of putatively efficient markets for central-bank stabilization-policies are harder to fathom.

At date t, the market would possess a complete description of central-bank actions relative to, contingent upon, external disturbances; an efficient Market would know more about the central bank than the Bank knew about itself! Variability would be imparted onto the Market only by events unpredictable by *anybody*. Thus, even if the central bank were exceptionally stupid or perverse so that it would contract the growth-rate of the monetary-base once it perceived that liquidity-preference had *increased*, the Market would immediately mark down securities prices once the event, *heightened liquidity preference,* became perceived, as it would be as rapidly as information-transmission constraints permitted. So it becomes clear that the performance of the economy clearly is not invariant against the properties of central-bank policy-making under efficient-market hypotheses. It remains appropriate under such hypotheses to devise optimal policy structures and hence to *choose* between policies.

Once a central bank had chosen a policy-structure—that is a complete set of actions relative to contingent events as well as the economy's structural parameters, as known to the Bank—it might become frustrated, if efficient markets prevailed, by a growing awareness that, once the Bank had locked in its policy-structure, security-market performance was dominated by external events, perhaps akin to random shocks but in any case unpredictable to anybody. As long as the Bank abjured wild play, as long as it did not *randomize* its strategy, it would have to live with such frustration. If markets are efficient, only a *fauve*, if not *fou*, Bank can move them.

Mechanical principles

There is a 'story' each month like that in the *Wall Street Journal* for 27 September 1976 and one each week like that in the *Journal* for 15 April 1977.

WSJ: 27 September 1976
The Federal Reserve Board's Open Market Committee voted at its Aug. 17 meeting to leave monetary policy unchanged between then and the September meeting held last Tuesday. According to records of the August meeting released Friday, the panel voted to continue aiming for a federal funds rate of $5\frac{1}{4}$ per cent and for growth in the so-called M-1 money supply of 4% to 8% annually and M-2 growth of $7\frac{1}{2}$% to $11\frac{1}{2}$% annually.

The panel's decisions are carried out through the buying and selling of securities in the open market, transactions that affect bank reserves. The interest rate on federal funds—the overnight reserves banks lend one another—is directly influenced by these transactions.

While the desired $5\frac{1}{4}$% rate on federal funds was left unchanged, the committee did vote in August to narrow the range in which the rate would be allowed to fluctuate. The new range is 5% to $5\frac{1}{2}$%; the old was $4\frac{3}{4}$% to $5\frac{3}{4}$%. At the July meeting, the committee widened the range, and the records of the August meeting indicate the members continued to hold conflicting views on the issue.

WSJ: 15 April 1977
Money supply posted surge in April 6 week increase in M1 was record at $5 billion; sharpness of gains causes surprise
... The big boost caused traders to cut prices, and raise yields, on short-term government securities, partly wiping out gains recorded earlier in the day after President Carter announced he was scrapping plans [for a tax rebate]...
... [s]pecialists worried that further large increases could spark the Fed to pull in its credit reins... That worry caused interest rates to rise
...

The 'stories' contain the lineaments of the Federal Reserve's bastard system of money-supply control. They need only be filled in.

Why 'bastard system'? Because the system ensues from an illicit doctrinal union of the schools of the New York and St. Louis Federal Reserve Banks, the latter here roughly coinciding with the views of Professor Milton Friedman. The New York school centres on *money-market conditions;* the St. Louis school on *money-supply performance.* Under a pure New York policy regime, money-supply performance would be what it must be in order for money-market conditions—substantially tracked by interest-rate behaviour and fairly well tracked by federal-funds rate alone—to be what the Federal Reserve wanted them to be. Under a pure St. Louis regime, money-market conditions would be what they must be for money-supply performance(s) to be what the Federal Reserve wanted it (them) to be. Under the prevailing regime, the open-market operator supplies federal-reserve credit to the market, or extracts federal-reserve credit from the market, from day to day depending upon whether the federal-funds rate is tending to rise above or fall below its targeted range. *But* the consequences for money-supply are closely monitored. If the upshot is an expansion-rate for money-supply—or, perhaps better, a weighted average of expansion-rates of variously-defined money-supplies—outside of the target range of money-supply expansion, there must be a re-think. The prevailing regime conflates criteria of the New York *and* St. Louis regimes. So it is a bastard—you may prefer 'mongrel'—regime.

The mongrel regime has provoked the emergence of a pseudo-science, *Federal Reserve watching;* cf. the *WSJ,* 15 April 1977, excerpt *supra.* Since the Federal Reserve wants to establish compatible target ranges for the funds-rate and for money-supply expansion, and since it does not control enough instruments to assure such compatibility, it adjusts to dissonant data-behaviour by changing its targets. *How* will it change its targets? Thus Federal Reserve watching.

The New York scheme looks the more plausible at first glance. Since response to changes in the time-path of supply of monetary reserves is indirect and, indeed, largely governed by perceived changes in interest rates, it seems natural for the Federal Reserve to formulate targets for interest rates or at least for so significantly representative a rate as the federal-funds rate. Alternatively, it might seem eccentric to focus on money-supply performance. The insentient particles of traditional economic theory are oblivious to money-supply; they choose money-holdings in the light of interest rates, wealth, levels of transactions activity, etc. And the sentient (rationally-expectational) particles, comprising the efficient markets of some recent theory, will be affected by money-supply developments only because of their implications for performance in the future of price indexes, interest rates, etc. In no case does correct theory contain direct linkage between the path of aggregate money-supply and 'micro' behaviour; the looseness of some monetarist discourse in this connection, apparently in order to promote proselytism, accordingly is the more regrettable.

Unfortunately, applied economic theory has not been able to ascertain what is the natural rate of interest now. And an important reason for this discomfiture, indeed a latent source of the dynamic instability of a pure New York regime, is the major, if rather inchoate, role of *inflation expectations*.

Say that the 'natural' federal-funds rate is 6 per cent, relative to some sort of consensus expectation of an inflation rate of 4 per cent per annum. Such a consensus would not be explicit; indeed it would become perceptible only quite long after the fact. Next say that the Federal Reserve thinks that the natural funds rate is 5 per cent; the Federal Reserve too will be wrong most of the time. In a New York regime the upshot will be suboptimal when not just about disastrous.

In the scenario just unfolded, the Federal Reserve would proceed to accelerate the rate of monetary expansion in order to bring down the funds rate; the Federal Reserve would be trying to force down the funds rate below its 'natural' level. Recalling from Chapter 2 how such a 'natural' level is defined, the upshot must be suboptimal: inflation will speed up; the growth of real activity will, if anything, be impaired.

As for *disaster*, expectations of accelerating inflation as reserves are injected more rapidly into the banking system will lead to a rising natural fund-rate, perhaps 8 per cent relative to an expected inflation-rate of 6 per cent. *But,* if the Federal Reserve holds its funds-rate target at 5 per cent, it will pump in reserves still faster. As inflation expectations burgeon, so will upward pressures on interest rates, including the funds rate; given interest rates will look more and more attractive to potential borrowers of depreciating money. So the gap between the target-rate and the actual-rate will grow as Federal Reserve credit is pumped into the system faster and faster—calling for still faster monetary expansion under a 'New York' rule. A vicious circle indeed! Nor is the scenario improbable (in the sense of the *Ars Poetica*): money-market conditions would be getting tighter as potential borrowers became more excited and potential lenders more wary.

The second *WSJ* excerpt makes up a perfect case study in efficient (rationally-expectational) markets. Interest rates rise *at once* because arbitrageurs[3] are stimulated to sell money short (to issue debt), putting the proceeds into 'pro-inflationary' assets, until interest rates properly reflect what is going to happen.

So reflection enhances the modest St. Louis/Friedman rule—steady, moderate monetary expansion by authorities eschewing discretion. Authorities in such a regime, tying themselves to the mast, albeit perhaps twitching to discretionary siren calls, block out destabilizing feedback. They act on the economy, but the economy then does not act on them. They cannot be effulgently successful. They cannot be disastrously wrong.

Minutiae

There follows an exegesis of the *Wall Street Journal* excerpts.

Federal funds are credits against the Federal Reserve. Often these funds are sold by banks with excess reserves to banks with deficient reserves; more exactly, by banks with undesired reserves to banks who desire more reserves. Federal Reserve open-market operations make an immediate impact on the funds rate. As Federal Reserve sales drain off reserves, there will be immediate excess demand for federal funds. Obviously, if the operator is instructed to push up the funds rate today, he will cut back the rate at which he has been supplying reserves to the system. There *is* a short-term equivalence in raising the funds rate to reducing the rate of growth of Federal Reserve credit, although the calibration of the force working from a shift in the funds-rate target to say contracted reserve-growth, let alone money-supply growth, is rough.

The transmission of the effects of changed funds-rate on the spectrum of interest rates is in principle very simple and in detail very complex. Thus higher funds-rate makes it more attractive for bankers to plan to liquidate assets in order to generate and then deploy excess federal funds. Higher funds-rate also makes plans to borrow federal funds look less profitable. So, throughout the system, offers to lend other than federal funds will shrink at prevailing interest rates. Pressures towards higher interest rates will project themselves into the full reach of the credit market.

The fact that Federal Reserve actions get transmitted to the economy through a chain of profit-motivated responses, beginning with those of the clearing banks, explains the exceptionally large slippages in the monetary base → money supply chain. This has been recognized for some time. James Meigs did a great deal, in 1962, to clarify the analysis.[4] Thus, for some time, stress was placed on *free reserves,* i.e. excess less borrowed reserves of the American clearing banks. This stress led to significant error in formulating criteria for Federal Reserve action. It was assumed that, when free reserves were falling, perhaps becoming more negative, the banks were under liquidity-pressure, that, on net, contractive pressure was being exerted on the banks. Then Meigs pointed out that the appropriate criterion was the difference between actual and (admittedly only notionally) desired reserve-and borrowing-positions. If free reserves were falling because banks found it profitable to borrow more from the Federal Reserve, the Federal Reserve erroneously would make such borrowing still easier if it employed a naive free-reserve criterion.

It is easy to build up plausible scenarios demonstrating slippage between Federal Reserve actions and banking-system response. One will suffice.

Wishing to induce ease, the Federal Reserve supplies reserves to the system at an accelerated rate by stepping up open-market security purchases. The funds rate falls. This makes bank borrowing from the Federal Reserve relatively less profitable. So banks repay some of their borrowings, thus feeding back into the Federal Reserve some of the reserve-resources the FR had fed to them. And, if commercial and industrial (C & I) loan-demand does not much increase as credit-costs begin to decline, what might be sharp declines in gilt-edged yield and bill rate could encourage banks to make additional repayments to the central bank.[5]

The scenario leads into another sort of slippage. To some extent, money supply variation, surely in the short run, will reflect fluctuations in demands for credit that lead banks to increase (decrease) their borrowings from the Federal Reserve and which could cause a Federal Reserve operating under a flawed criterion to increase (decrease) the growth-rate of unborrowed reserves in counterproductive ways. In either case, the Federal Reserve then would be reacting 'pro-cyclically' to events in the economy it is supposed to regulate.

There are many examples in economic history of central banks, operating with incorrect decision rules, turning themselves into receivers instead of transmitters of controlling impulses and so promoting cumulative inflations or deflations. One thinks of the 'Weimar' inflation in Germany[6] or the sharp contraction of American money supply *circa* 1931–33.[7]

Completing discussion of how loan demand by bank customers can, over *some* length of run, cause 'reverse' or 'upstream' impulses to upset central-bank strategies,[8] if bank customers were to intensify their demands for loans, banks would begin to seek out additional resources to support expanded C & I lending. One such resource is federal funds. The funds rate would rise. And surely the curve describing bank-demand for borrowings at the Federal Reserve will shift rightwards; additional borrowings will lead to multiplied expansion of monetary aggregates in very well known ways. *And* if the Federal Reserve, operating in its contemporary (mongrel) mode, were slow to revise its target-range for fund rate, it might increase the target range for money-supply expansion, believing that money-supply targets had become too restrictive. The Federal Reserve then would fuel the 'needs of trade', pursuing the fallacy that dominated its founders and that dogged it long afterwards, with disastrous consequence.[9]

A quite clear-cut theme has emerged. Real-world monetary authorities, working with imperfect data inserted into crude models, easily can find themselves reacting to instead of acting on the economic processes they presume to control; real-world authorities easily can fall into pro-cyclical action so that they intensify rather than abate economic fluctuations. A 'New York' (money-market-conditions orientated) approach encourages 'pro-cyclical' bias; a simplistic, but surely unidirectional 'St. Louis' rule averts pro-cyclical bias.

Euro-market-related problems

Certain distortions develop from euro-banking phenomena analysed in Chapter 5. Thus loan statistics, especially for New York banks, can get distorted—without money-supply statistics beings affected. A second force affects both kinds of statistics, at least if *money supply* is interpreted in a certain way.

New York—or other—banks may prefer to book some loans at Cayman Island, Singapore or other branches instead of at head offices. The explanation usually can be extracted from the myriad of American banking regulations; offshore loans often can be written up more attractively. The statistical consequences of such placements are obvious. And Federal Reserve policies geared to money-market conditions might consequently become distorted: if the open-market committee thinks that loan-demand is sluggish, when all that has happened is that Cayman Island bookings have replaced New York bookings, the Federal Reserve might try to make money easier at the wrong time.

If a cheque against Continental Illinois bank is deposited, for dollar credit, with Crédit Lyonnais at Balbec, excess supply of dollar loans would develop as Crédit Lyonnais then moved to expand its dollar-asset portfolio. The (re)disintermediation analysis of Chapter 2 made this clear. And the euro-currency analysis of Chapter 5 shows that the upshot will *not* affect conventional measurements of U.S. monetary aggregates. The question we now briefly examine is:

> do the conventionally measured U.S. monetary aggregates—excluding, as they do, euro-dollar deposits and broadly meant to exclude dollar holdings of alien entities—make sense relative to sophisticated economic theory?

The answer is sharply *negative*. But its thrust is muffled by the fact that even perfectly measured monetary aggregates cannot correctly be perceived as directly influencing the economy. This is easy to see: any economic particle can hold as much money, or as many peanuts, as its wealth position makes feasibly desirable; so it seems to any economic particle. And the *indirect* consequences of changes in expansion rates of say dollar-denominated bank deposits are the same whether these are domestic or euro-accounts: it makes no difference for money-market conditions whether Crédit Lyonnais or Manufacturers Hanover is seeking to place what are for it augmented resources in dollar-credit markets.

Minutiae: money and credit

It is useful to develop further the distinction between money and credit. If a higher funds-rate is brought about by slowing down the rate at which reserves are created, then *ipso facto* the rate of monetary expansion will slow down: the contractive effects of slower expansion of un-borrowed reserves will be augmented by the fact that banks will want to reduce the reserves they borrow from each other when funds-rate is higher. (We have seen, however, that, if the Federal Reserve discount-rate is not simultaneously put up, banks will have greater incentive to borrow reserves from the Federal Reserve.) These might be called *impact effects*.

Continuing effects of a higher funds-rate on money and credit are of a different piece. Demand for M-1 will be less because of higher interest rates. But demand for *certificates of deposit,* for example, will basically be unaffected: CDs will carry higher rates; there will be no incentive to sub-stitute against them.[10] Indeed, if we assume that all 'money' is interest-bearing so that—pending contractive effects of higher interest rates on real activity and hence on *transactions demand for money*—quantities of money demanded may not be at all affected by higher funds-rate if all yields simply are bumped up.

The analysis has become congested and should be smoothed out.

First distinguish between quantum changes and changes in time-derivatives. A car might go at 40 miles per hour, stop dead for one hour and then continue at 40 m.p.h. At the end of one hour of travel, 40 miles had been accomplished; the odometer registered a quantum change of 40 miles. During the pause, there was *no* quantum change. The one-hour pause having ended, the speedometer would, upon the accelerator being pushed and various frictions and inertia being overcome, register 40 m.p.h.; the time-derivative displayed by the speedometer will have regained the '40' mark. If the car goes on long enough at 40 m.p.h., the stoppage will look like a mere blip in the line drawn in distance/time space.

Returning to the funds-rate scenario, and assuming that the percen-tage rate of growth of 'M' had been steady for some while, note that we have established that money-growth will be depressed while funds-rate is being pushed up; over, say, the first week of the new funds-rate, the quantum-change in money will be less than that of the previous week.

Under our stipulations, and pending the response of the real economy to higher interest rates, the key elements will be the banks and the money-holding public. The public will not be willing to hold the securities sold by the Federal Reserve, reducing their debt to banks by an amount determined by the *money multiplier* at the same time, *unless* in-terest rates paid on money (monies) fall relative to other rates.

The process implanting a higher funds-rate requires that the relative yield from money-holding fall; the market must be induced to make the substitutions of non-monetary for monetary assets required by the open-market sales that initially pushed up funds-rate. During the equivalent to the one-hour car-stoppage, the proportions or ratios describing financial holdings were altered.

A similar analysis would be made for the automobile sub-economy if the Government were to sell larger cars from its fleet, while buying smaller cars, in the open market.

Now consider *future growth* of money and other things; consider the equivalent to restoration of regular 40 m.p.h. car-motion. There is no reason why steady growth of the various sorts of financial paper would not resume so that the new proportions would be sustained. In principle, money-growth would continue at its old rate.

Summarizing, we have established that the quantum reduction in fresh money-creation over the implementation (of higher funds-rate) interval was but incidental to the reconstitution of the matrix of claims necessary to make feasible higher yields on non-monetary relative to monetary assets. That being done, credit expansion within the reconstituted claims-matrix could continue. Indeed it would be necessary for monetary expansion to proceed apace with general credit-expansion if the new claims matrix were to sustain its proportions. (We neglect interaction with the real economy here.)

Minutiae: topic, money measures

The money-supply measure, M-1, is not interesting in correct economic theory. And M-2, M-3, . . . are mixtures of quite heterogeneous substances, some being interest-bearing, others being non-interest-bearing. Still, order can be imposed upon the material.

(1) The controlling theoretical concept concerns the way in which micro-holdings of money are entirely endogenous for the economy's portfolio managers; each *chooses* his holdings of various assets and his issues of various liabilities. These choices are affected by absolute and relative levels of interest-rates, real rates of economic growth, etc.

In traditional texts on monetary economics the upshot has been elegantly simple. The central bank takes a decision on the instrument, reserve base. This decision determines the amount of bank-money through the bank-money multiplier. Then price levels and interest rates must change until the public want to hold the appropriate amount of money.

More-advanced models take account of slippage related to the public's propensity to hold currency; currency-holdings absorb part of the reserve base.

Narrowly-defined monetary aggregates slip and slide as monetary-base growth-rates change. And the reserve-base is absorbed by a number of kinds of clearing-bank deposits as well. When money-market conditions get tight, so that interest rates rise, current-account (demand deposit) growth falters while time-deposits accelerate relative to demand-deposits. Only very broadly defined monetary aggregates move even roughly in phase with the monetary base.

(2) Until quite recently, it seemed obvious that accelerated expansion of broad monetary aggregates, reflecting that of the monetary base, would generate excess liquidity leading to excess supply of credit (excess demand for securities) and hence (sic!) lower interest rates. Money markets now belie such a conjecture: securities prices fall when money supply accelerates and rise when it decelerates. Why? Because rationally expectational traders, anticipating the inflationary consequences of accelerated monetary expansion and acting as quasi-arbitrageurs, promptly bring yield curves into line with expectations of nominal profitabilities of activities; yield curves have become highly sensitive to inflation-expectations.

(3) It remains true that, whatever inflation-expectations are, accelerated expansion of the monetary base will provoke balance-sheet disequilibria. (There is a nice comparison possible here between effects of accelerated and unaccelerated expansion; cf. comparisons in physics based on effects of accelerated and non-accelerated motions; the latter are consistent with the same sorts of state-invariances as appear in analogous circumstances in economic theory.) Thus banks will probe out in all directions, seeking profitable drains of excess resources; true, the banks will offer these funds at higher, not lower, nominal interest rates, but inflation expectations will increase borrowers' proposed yields concomitantly.

(3) and (1) are in nice apposition. The liquidity-reduction process described in (3) works its way out in financial markets; the public do not feel wealthier because of Federal Reserve purchases; they do not splurge. The liquidity-reduction process becomes accompanied, perhaps very quickly under the expectational conditions of modern markets, by price-inflation. Each member of the public, always able—as he perceives things— to hold whatever 'M' he wants to hold, subject to his wealth and borrowing power, unwittingly contributes towards achievement of the equilibrium he finally nests in.

(4) In terms of the pragmatic criteria that must control monetary-policy choices in so crude a science, authorities in the end will focus on monetary aggregates that, *when properly measured,* are most predictably linked with variables like nominal GNP. It follows that relative ease of

accurate prompt measurement will affect the choice of the 'key' monetary aggregate.

Say that the authorities find that the monetary aggregate, M_s best tracks nominal GNP; call that y. This means that the path of v_s, where

$$M_s v_s = y$$

at any time, is optimally predictable.[11] So the Federal Reserve's open-market committee would, in the prevailing mongrel regime, instruct the open-market operator to keep M_s within designated ranges so long as funds-rate were within its designated range, etc.

(5) The framework just built supports a striking comparison between simplistic monetarist and anti-monetarist positions. A radically anti-monetarist economist might predict that the track of y was independent of that of M_s so that the only effect of M_s deviations was on the track of v_s. Indeed the *liquidity-trap* discussion of Chapters 2 and 7, rooted in parts of Keynes's *General Theory*, could be structured in just this way.

4 Money Supply Control in the U.K.

4.1 The pre-1971 system; before 'Competition and Credit Control'

The British debate on money-supply theory contains several layers, all confused. In the wake of Keynes's *General Theory* (1936), many economists, admittedly able to cite some extravagant *GT* language, maintained that money-supply was irrelevant to, say, price-performance because monetary velocity was infinitely malleable; prices, they argued, were determined by properties of wage-bargains and by the curve of investment expenditures; the level of nominal national expenditure thus becoming determined, velocity became a function of money-supply; the greater was money supply, the less would be monetary velocity. This view became predominant in the British Treasury and indeed has only quite recently lost force in Great George Street.

So at one level of debate it was argued that it did not matter what was the supply of money. And, indeed, money-supply statistics probably intruded forcibly into British economic-political life only when overseeing teams from the I.M.F. rather humiliatingly began to keep watch over British policy under loan agreements in the late 1960s. And, reflecting what has been a lot of bad economic luck in post-war Britain, the I.M.F. invigilators brought a modern form of an old fallacy—going back to the Currency School—into the heart of British policy-making: Domestic Credit Expansion (DCE). It is assumed in Chapter 4 that monetary velocity is not infinitely malleable, so that money-supply behaviour does matter. This modest assertion now is widely supported in Britain. Support would be more massive today and would have developed earlier if Britain did not have so many brilliant economists able to build plausible cases against common sense.

The next level of debate has concerned the proximate determinants of money-supply and has been conducted in a dense fog because most participants get confused between monetary expansion and various sorts of credit expansion. This segment of the monetary debate can be organized into two subsections. One, the source of most of the work done in this chapter, revolves about more or less mechanical considerations; thus Section 4.1 mostly deals with the pre-1971 debate on the relative importance of the cash- and liquidity-ratios or the counterpart cash-base and liquid-asset-supply concepts. This sub-debate became resolved, one is tempted to say, 'naturally', in favour of the fallacious liquidity-ratio side in 1971. The other subsection hinges upon a rather subtle connotation of the notion of exercising *control* in economic policy, upon the 'true' meaning of *exogenous* in economic parlance. It is briefly taken up immediately below.

Some British commentators allow that the authorities can get a firm grip on money-supply. *But,* they go on to argue, in the actual socio-economic working out of the system, money-supply becomes determined by wage-bargains and, some of them also contend, by the behaviour of administered prices in the industrial and service sectors. More specifically, it is commonly alleged that concern about unemployment and prolonged stagnation in the growth of national output typically will force the government of the day to *validate* wage increases imposed by powerful unions in some sectors and then felt by other sectors in the form of cost-push pressures. *Validation* would take the form of accelerated monetary expansion, if the wage increases in fact were 'excessive'. This is not the place to offer a treatise on so diffuse a subject, but some remarks on the underlying premisses can be made: the argument is bottomed on the assumption that British labour either is peculiarly irrational or singularly unpatriotic.

Rational unions would establish *real-wage* targets and proceed to bargain within a context established by monetary policy, surely including the course of monetary expansion. If the time-path of the money-supply became thoroughly established so that, under admittedly quite rigidly monetarist stipulations, the path of nominal national product became correspondingly defined, unions could frame demands with clear *real* implications. Under these circumstances, there would be no reason for rational, socially-congenial (that is not revolutionary) trade unionists to frame demands that they know would be 'validated' only by inflationary monetary issue; such demands are not on their face calculated to promote trade-unionist interests. It seems more plausible that some of the undoubtedly *fauve* union demands of recent years have more flowed from an inflationary environment determined by exceptionally high rates of monetary expansion than they have contributed to that inflation: knowing that collective bargaining leads to sticky wages (the periodicity of the negotiations makes that almost certain), trade unionists have wanted to *anticipate* inflation.

It was established in Chapter 2 that there no longer is perceived to be a simple trade-off between inflation and unemployment. Thus if real wage rates were to increase quite abruptly by say 15 per cent, and if monetary policy proved completely unresponsive, it is indeed almost certain that unemployment would increase: many activities would become unprofitable and consequently be abandoned; although investment in some labour-saving machinery would be stimulated, investment would on the whole be discouraged by the erosion of profit margins; falling share prices would discourage much expenditure. And a sort of conventional wisdom argues that a responsive monetary policy would mitigate consequences for unemployment: higher rates of price inflation would erode the real-wage gains. This 'conventional wisdom' is specious: it is rooted in a *petitio principii*. The crucial question, begged by the 'conventional wisdom', concerns trade-union power: are the unions, or are they not, powerful enough to claw in a 15 per cent increase in *real* wage rates? And, if they know that they are not that powerful, why would they not finally settle for the most that they know the political-economic-social power-structure *in toto* will allow them? In any case, to argue that the trade unionists naively would accept, year after year, erosion of their bargaining gains by a sort of counter-attacking inflationary monetary policy without accelerating their demands is to impose a dumb-beast stipulation about them and to deny the force of *rational-expectations* reasoning very blatantly indeed.

The *wages-and-inflation* nexus just explored is a fertile hunting ground for rational-expectations theory; the problems are peculiar to a social subject; the disastrous consequences so far of adherence to the 'conventional wisdom' cannot be surprising to masters of economic logic.

Cash-Ratios and Liquidity-Ratios Before Spring 1971

The *cash-ratio* was a characteristically informal, but practically binding, requirement that British clearing banks hold balances at the Bank of England and vault cash equal to at least *eight per cent* of their deposit liabilities. (*Special-deposit* requirements were above and beyond the cash-ratio constraint.) It bears obvious similarity to the American reserve requirements discussed in Chapter 3. And, if this analogy indeed held up—or holds up—analyses hinging on Bank of England credit would lead to the same, broadly favourable, conclusions about the ability of the British authorities to control monetary growth as those reached about the American system. The *histoire* is typical of postwar British economic experience. The analogy does hold up. A New Orthodoxy, culminating with the *Radcliffe Report* (1959), was able to convince all but a few that the analogy was false. The 1971 'reform' further strengthened the 'New Orthodox' position, granting that, as the Bank has become more committed to establishing a grip on money-supply, its practice has become increasingly sensitive to the old wisdom.

The attack on the use of the cash-ratio as a prime instrument is succinctly supported in a yellowing article by two American experts of the time. 'The cash ratio does not serve as an independent limitation on the supply of bank credit because, as long as the Bank of England continues its traditional practice of serving as a lender of last resort, the banks can translate other liquid assets into cash by calling loans to the discount houses and forcing the market into the Bank.'[1] The argument is invalid for the same reason that the attack on the cash-base as an instrument was invalid: since Bank Rate was *penal,* the discount houses, and hence the market as a whole, would be in disequilibrium as long as they were in the Bank (as long as they were taking credit from the Bank at Bank Rate); this disequilibrium would persist until the houses had repaid the Bank, thus draining off as much Bank of England credit as had been elicited by clearing-bank calls of loans to the market; the 'old wisdom' was valid so long as Bank Rate was penal, something that never would have been denied.

The constraint-system before 1971 was in fact rather complex. Banks came to be expected to maintain a *liquidity ratio* of at least 30 per cent (in time this requirement became flexible, the idea being that there should be created a monetary equivalent to the then much-admired Chancellor's Regulator). Eligible liquid assets included vault cash, balances at the Bank of England, money at call or at less than seven days' notice and certain commercial-bills, along with Treasury-bills. These eligible liquid assets were expected (by the authorities) to be equal in value to at least 30 per cent of the net deposit obligation of the clearing banks. The liquidity-ratio concept emerged from some prudential notions that were quite irrelevant to the liquidity of the banking system as a whole: the *system* could not raise legal tender by selling assets unless the Bank were willing to supply these funds. Central banking theory is cluttered with vestigial remnants of schemes of prudential regulations formed before modern money-supply-control regimes were thought of.

Two jobs remain to be done. (1) We want to see how it was that so much attention became focused on liquidity-ratios. (2) We want to see why a system of money-supply control rooted in a liquidity-ratio concept would be inefficient; it has become clear already that the upshot is important for the study of post-1971 experience.

Why did liquidity ratios get to look so important? It was incorrectly thought that the cash-base was a faulty lever, that clearing banks could transform discount-market credit into Bank of England credit. The exchange would be of one liquid asset for another; clearing banks would not thus replenish their eligible liquid assets; the broader measure would be unaffected by substitutions between components.

We shall see that it is quite easy for clearing banks to 'make' liquid assets. They can buy bills with the proceeds of sales of long assets. They can reduce loans, increasing eligible commercial bills. The creators of the New Orthodoxy knew of these possibilities, but assumed them away. Then they treated the artificial residue as if it were the real world.

Why are money-supply-control systems based on liquidity-ratios inefficient? They violate the controlling proposition of banking theory: so long as clearing-bank reserves comprise central-bank credit, the Bank can control the reserve base as would a ratchet-wheel; the diffusive reserve system, based on the liquidity-ratio and implemented in 1971, loosens the link between Bank action and clearing-bank reserve-positions. (The argument must be slightly refined if the clearing-bank/discount-house nexus is to be reflected.)

The slackness in money-supply control caused by implementation of the liquidity-ratio concept has tacitly been recognized: the *special deposit* device has become important in British practice.

Special deposits developed from credit restraints imposed in 1960 and first became important during the 1961 squeeze, a response to a balance-of-payments 'crisis'. Special deposits, maintained by the clearing banks with the Bank of England, do not count against reserve requirements. Special-deposit requirements originally were defined relative to banks' deposit liabilities; since quite recently, as part of yet another 'innovation', the 'Corset', bank-asset expansion, if too rapid, can lead to calls for special deposits.

So long as there was a binding and independent cash-ratio requirement, the special-deposit mechanism was quite different in practice than it seemed to be at first glance. The reason becomes obvious upon asking, 'what would be the *source* of special deposits?' Stipulating that there are binding and independent cash-ratio requirements, if Clearing Bank A is to make a special deposit, it either must put up vault cash (this can be put aside) or attract funds from Clearing Bank B; the *system* of banks could not generate additional central-bank credit. So a special-deposit requirement could be satisfied only in two ways: (1) bank liabilities could contract; (2) the Bank could supply the wherewithal for special deposits.

The first modality, so far as I know, was not employed. It would have been harsh: there would have had to have been roughly a £12 contraction in bank asset-portfolios for each £1 in special deposits that was called for.

The second modality fed into the developing suzerainty of the liquidity-ratio mechanism, fulfilled in 1971. In order to acquire what were in fact tranches of fresh Bank-of-England credit, the banks would have to sell assets; put differently, the fresh central-bank credit, roughly equal to the fresh special-deposit requirement, was supplied through open-market purchases by the authorities. To the extent that liquid assets thus were sold by banks, a credit squeeze would have been put into force. And, indeed, there were sound 'technical' reasons to assume that, preponderantly, the banks would sell short-dated rather than long-dated stock.[2]

The pre-1971 system was in fact *not* one of *money-supply* control; rather it attempted to affect rates of *credit expansion*. British policy became formulated in terms of money-supply only under duress from the I.M.F.

and, then, the upshot was ill-articulated.

Readers wishing to pursue Section 4.1 farther, thus incidentally gripping still more tightly the predominance of liquidity-ratio-based thinking in Britain, will study in some depth a topic that was called *disinflation by funding*.[3] (This gimmick enjoyed great play in the United States at the same time.)

The *aggregate* supply of liquid assets obviously will be affected by the proportion of public debt represented by short-dated instruments, importantly including Treasury Bills to the total or, of course, to the amount of *funded* public debt (*Consols* represented funding à *outrance*; gilt-edged stock is funded). To the extent that funded debt is substituted say for Bills by the Treasury, the aggregate supply of liquid assets will fall. And if, following the sort of model projected by Dacey, a model that enjoyed wide support despite its crudity, we assumed that the non-banking public were inflexible in its Bill-holding choices,[4] it would follow that the banks would find themselves short of liquid assets: the discount market would take off less bank-money; the total of Bills available to the banks for direct purchase would be less. Then the banks would be forced to contract their advances, etc. In fact, the public's elasticity of substitution for stocks of various dates proved to be quite high; *disinflation by funding* lives on, surprisingly robustly, only because of the characteristically Bourbon quality of 'establishment' monetary thinking.

4.2 The new regime; Competition and Credit Control, 1971

As any reader of the Bank of England's Economic Intelligence Unit's definitive *Competition and Credit Control* (covering material published in the Bank's *Quarterly Bulletin* from 1971 to 1975) readily will ascertain, the reforms announced by the Governor in May 1971 covered a number of fields. Our treatment of the material will be both partial and stylized. We shall centre on the keen analogy between the reformed system and what we called in Chapter 3 the 'New York' school of money-supply control (if a point of view so orientated towards the condition of credit can be called one towards money-supply control). Taking due account of the enhanced role for special deposits, we shall show why money-supply is apt to continue to be difficult to control in a system so rooted in 'credit' and so committed to a highly-flawed liquidity-ratio-like criterion; in such a system money-supply tends to become a function of the demand for credit! The special-deposit mechanism is intended to thwart this tendency but, even under the best practical circumstances, officials cannot hope to be nimble enough to deploy it powerfully enough to offset the system's inherent flaws. The subsection is concluded with a discussion of British money-supply measures, including DCE.

How 'money' is led by 'credit' under 'Competition and Credit Control'; the 'Corset'

Our theme concerns a certain perverse ingenuity that has dogged monetary-policy formation in Britain for some time and which contrasts so sharply with the brilliant success enjoyed by the City, unrivalled in its suppleness.

The *eligible-reserve-asset* and *special-deposit* concepts should be put into play at once.

> ELIGIBLE RESERVE ASSETS will comprise balances with the Bank of England (other than special deposits), British government and Northern Ireland government Treasury bills, company tax reserve certificates, money at call with the London money market, British government stocks with one year or less to final maturity, local authority bills ... and (up to a maximum of 2 per cent of eligible liabilities) commercial bills eligible for rediscount at the Bank of England. (*Competition and Credit Control*, p. 10.)

Special deposits already have been defined. But it is useful to explain the 17 December 1973 extension of the special-deposit mechanism to attempts to control the pace of bank lending; as well as explaining the 'Corset' mechanism, the material just below inadvertently reveals how dominant is the credit-control aspect, how subordinate is money-supply proper, in the *CCC*/1971 system.

> ... the Bank announced ... [that the] banks and finance houses have agreed [!] individually to place non-interest-bearing supplementary deposits with the Bank if the interest-bearing eligible liabilities ... grow faster than a specified rate...
>
> The rate of growth of interest-bearing liabilities depends in part upon the rates of interest offered by the banks. Strong bidding for funds by the banks ... could result in their eligible liabilities rising faster than the allowable rate, and thus incurring a progressively larger penalty ... The arrangements should therefore restrain the pace of monetary expansion, including the pace at which the banks [expand loans], without requiring rises in short-term interest rates and bank lending rates to unacceptable heights. (*Competition and Credit Control*, p. 10)

In order to understand the sequel, it is important to deepen an analysis begun in Chapter 3; there may be no more difficult 'knot' in the whole field of financial policy; even distinguished financial journalists often get *money* and *credit* mixed up.

When journalists say, 'demand for money has become stronger', they mean that demand for *finance* has increased; would-be borrowers do not usually intend, other than transitorily, to use loan-proceeds to increase their monetary balances. When economists say, 'demand for money has increased', they mean that the public plan to increase their holdings of say currency and current accounts (M-1).

How does one intend to increase one's monetary balances? Usually by cutting back spending (including capital spending) or by selling assets (granted that creating a liability is like selling an asset). If households attempt to increase their monetary balances, they are especially apt to cut back on the accumulation of consumer-durables.

The appearance of things encourages the common confusion between money and credit: if the demand for finance should increase, there will be excess supply of securities; if the demand for money should increase, there will be excess supply of securities.

We now are prepared to study how monetary balances will grow in phase with the demand for credit if authorities do—as do the British authorities—key on the condition of credit. Thus assume that the monetary authorities decide that the appropriate level of interest rates is one keyed to a Minimum Lending Rate (MLR) of 9 per cent. And then assume that demand for credit (finance) becomes strong. The authorities, and most media commentators, are apt to refer to the importance of assuring that ample credit is available to finance the burgeoning expansion in the economy; in equivalent American circumstances, Congressmen will espy Federal Reserve caution threatening to choke off the expansion.

It was established in Chapter 2 that the hypothetical commentaries would be *incorrect*: the proper job of the monetary authorities is to satisfy liquidity preference, i.e. demand for money proper, not to supply credit. The reason is simple: the monetary authorities *cannot* provide real resources; real resources are supplied by real saving.

The consequences of confusion of money and credit are not minor. The authorities, thinking that they were supplying 'real' finance, would in fact be pumping up the money stock. And the banks themselves easily could be unaware of the truth of the matter: although banks essentially operate a revolving fund of credit, they easily can perceive themselves as lending out 'resources' flowing in as a result of what Marshall called 'abstinence'. In truth, to the extent that banks are able to expand their credits, by somehow augmenting their liquid-asset bases, when an economy is effectively fully employed (recall how easy it is for an economy to be in that state; cf. Chapter 2), all that happens is that excess demands for various 'real' goods become financed by undesired monetary issues—undesired until consequent inflation increases demand for nominal balances, as it does, short of a hyperinflationary phase. *If credit can expand elastically as demand for finance expands, money-supply will be dragged up by the credit-expansion willy-nilly.*

Turning to the post-1971 British system in some detail, there is, in any moderate length of run, no firm monetary base; indeed the banking system's stock of eligible liquid assets will tend to move sympathetically with credit-demand; when demand for finance accelerates, banks, and similar financial institutions, will acquire Treasury bills directly from the public and will expand loans to the discount houses, thus indirectly acquiring commercial and Treasury bills; direct acquisition of commercial bills will become attractive; etc. The upshot is reminiscent of the flaws in American Federal-Reserve management, again causing money-supply growth to respond elastically to credit demand and provoking the disastrous monetary contractions of 1931–33; the deep-rooted heretical source is the Banking School of the nineteenth century and its Real Bills doctrine.

The abstracts from *Competition and Credit Control* (1971) show that the Bank is conscious of the risks posed by the elasticity of the eligible-reserve-asset base. Its response has been to employ the *special-deposits* mechanism more vigorously, partly by extending it to the 'Corset' policy.

If the authorities discover that credit is expanding 'too rapidly', pushing up monetary-growth as a result, they might call for special deposits, thus immobilizing part of what in the past would have been called the cash base. So long as the banks are not bound by an implicit or informal equivalent to the .old cash-ratio, they can at least partially counteract the need to put up more special deposits by acquiring still more bills, directly or indirectly. However, calls for special deposits surely will have *some* braking effect.

We have become familiar with the *lags* that both control and impede discretionary monetary policy. It takes time to find out what is happening; it takes more time to formulate a response; it takes still more time for the response to be put into operation; it takes still more time for the effects of the counter-operations to take hold and yet longer for the authorities to learn what these effects have been. And the whole process can become destabilized if its *feedback* channels are not, so to speak, damped. The 'Corset', described by the excerpt from *CCC* (1971), p. 29, comprises sort of a pre-setting of the control mechanism. Or one might go further and say that, by December 1973, the authorities had become sufficiently worried about the inherent flaw in their system, i.e. by the elasticity of the eligible-reserve-asset base, that they brought in 'monetarism' through the back door. But the result is a puny monetarism; much depends upon the pace at which banks generate additional eligible assets able to substitute for Bank credit sterilized by fresh special-deposit requirements. Indeed the *raison d'être* of the 'Corset' is anti-monetarist: it is based on the fear that conventionally monetarist restraint could cause interest rates to rise 'unacceptably'. At best, the 'Corset' merely increases the implicit cost of marginal resources for banks at times when demand for finance and inflation-expectations both are accelerating; such a deterrent is apt to be ineffectual.

Chapters 2, 3 and 4 repeatedly conclude that monetary policy ought to be about money, not credit: monetary authorities supply liquid claims but are positioned outside the process transforming real savings into real investment. Why then are national authorities so reluctant to define monetary policy in terms of 'money'? Because of the *politics* of interest rates: it is feared that, under a monetarist rule, interest rates may rise 'too much' if accelerated demands for finance collide with the Rule; it is forgotten that to try to push down the nominal rate of interest when the equilibrium real-rate is rising only will make the equilibrium nominal rate rise still more as inflation-expectations are inflamed.[5]

Money-supply measures: M-1, M-3 and Domestic Credit Expansion

M-1 is defined as notes and coin in circulation with the public plus sterling current accounts held within the private sector, and M-3 is defined as all deposits held with the United Kingdom banking sector by United Kingdom residents in the public and private sectors, plus notes and coin. Loosely speaking, M-1 is non-interest-bearing money and M-3 is that plus interest-bearing money.[6]

The analysis is so obviously within the confines of similar American measures, so exhaustively studied in Chapter 3, that we can confine our M-1/M-3 discussion to some remarks about *roundtripping*.

A *round-trip* finds a bank's client more or less simultaneously borrowing 'money' from the bank and purchasing a certificate of deposit issued by a bank; *roundtripping* is an arbitrage transaction, reflecting CD rates higher than lending rates to prime borrowers. (Such differentials are not always present.) At times in recent years, roundtripping has led to massive distortions in monetary statistics: at times M-3 has increased very sharply simply because of roundtripping.

It was promptly perceived all round that such increases in the stock of money involved simultaneous increases in supply and demand, that it would be improper to infer that excess liquidity was thus being generated. Put differently, such increases in the stock of money are associated, almost 1:1, with decreased monetary velocity. The upshot had to be distressing for monetarists, but it did not undermine monetarism. Why?

Monetarists would make inelastic the behaviour of the monetary base; then there would be no way for M-3 to leap ahead, fuelled by increases in the eligible-reserve asset-base manufactured by the banks. Roundtripping is one of the facets of the elastic or malleable reserve-base inherent in the *CCC* (1971) programme.

Domestic Credit Expansion (DCE)

'In broad terms, the amount of "domestic credit expansion" in a given period is equivalent to the increase in domestic money stock after adjustment for any change in money balances caused directly by an external surplus or deficit.'[7] The grey official language masks a quite dramatic, and eccentric, implication for financial policy: the adjustment is in reverse. So measured DCE is increased by an external deficit and reduced by a surplus. Accordingly, if monetary policy were to be governed by a DCE criterion, and if some norm had come to be established relative to *balanced* payments, M-1 or M-3, as conventionally conceived, would grow less rapidly *pari passu* with an external deficit and more rapidly *pari passu* with an external surplus. Monetary policy would become sensitized to the balance of payments. The Currency School would become restored.

Recall the doctrine of the Currency School. The behaviour of money-supply was supposed to imitate what would have been the case if 'money' were metallic; then external deficits would lead 1:1 to decreases in what otherwise would have been the stock of money. Then monetary expansion would follow a course independent of the *needs of trade*; the apposition to the doctrine of the Banking School was complete.

It suffices here to point out that it can make absolutely no sense simultaneously to float the pound, however dirtily, and to make monetary policy sensitized to a Rule that can make sense only relatively to support of rigidly fixed foreign-exchange rates. Under DCE 'logic', British monetary policy would become pro-cyclical. Then Britain would inflate as its trade-balance improved and deflate as it deteriorated. An improving trade-balance leads to a fall in measured DCE and a deteriorating one to a rise; relative to a fixed DCE target, an improving trade balance would call for further expansion in DCE, etc.

There is a political *raison d'être* of a sort for 'DCE': when the British trade balance was so heavily adverse, DCE supplied cover for the politically difficult task of curbing money-growth, partly because it was convenient for the government of the day to blame the IMF. But there is no proper analytical apologia: the effect of imposing DCE upon a prudent monetary rule is to contract the rate of liquid-asset expansion as aggregate demand decays and expand it when aggregate demand waxes.

4.3 Public Sector Deficits, Monetary Expansion and the Balance of Payments

4.3.1 The Public Sector Deficit and Money Supply

Not only laymen have become confused about the relationship between public-sector deficits (PSDs) and money-supply. Indeed there is a flimsy analytical tie; the substantial relationship is political, and it reflects the bias towards 'cheap money' of democratic politics.

Before Keynes's theory became influential, any orthodox economist would have said that public-sector deficits could be financed by higher taxes, by borrowing in the money markets or by the central bank. The second choice concerns 'non-inflationary borrowing' and has been exhaustively studied in Chapter 2 (cf. 'Crowding out'). By some quirk, it has become taken for granted that the third choice, inflationary borrowing, *naturally* accompanies PSDs.

It was established in Chapter 2 that, if substantial resource-slackness exists, public-sector deficits can be self-financing; Keynes's theory can be said to start from that point. Section 4.3 is built on the assumption that there is effectively-full employment of resources; the justification for this assumption again is in Chapter 2.

There is a valid, if limited, sense in which PSDs *do* induce concomitant increases in money-supply—just as a surge in loan demand will lead to at least a temporary increase in money supply in anything but a perfectly inelastic system of money-supply control, i.e. a system completely without feedback. Thus, upon the PSD *increasing,* official monetary balances would become chequed into private balances, thus augmenting M-3. And local authorities would be likely to increase their bank-credit-taken just as would private borrowers when they increase *their* cash deficits. And we have seen that, in the prevailing British system, increased demand for credit leads to increased monetary growth quite directly.

Surely the most perverse, and perhaps the most pervasive, fallacy in modern political economy is the proposition that the central bank can, *in general,* reduce equilibrium real interest rates by expanding the monetary base more rapidly. Of course, this fallacy lies behind the virtual consensus that massive PSDs, unaccompanied by accelerated monetary growth, would lead to 'unacceptably high rates of interest'. The truth, developed in Chapter 2, is that, in recent years, nominal British interest rates would have been lower if money-growth had not been so fast: inflation-premiums then would have been much lower. And the truth is that the only effective way that the official sector could have driven down real rates of interest, without clogging incentives further with still higher taxes, would have been to have cut back the growth of public expenditure. One more effort will be made here to drive home these 'truths'.

Perhaps the proximate cause for so much confusion about money-growth and interest rates lies in the fact that operational, actual markets determine *nominal, not real,* interest rates. The 'market' determining real interest rates is a notional one: disequilibrium in that 'market' cannot be observed directly; only its consequences permit such disequilibrium to be inferred. Furthermore, in the evocative French locution, *liquides* can be poured onto the operational market so as to hold down, for a time, nominal interest rates: for example, the authorities, backed by their 'printing press', simply could stand ready to buy paper on an X per cent yield basis; the yield would not rise above X per cent. But at least one other thing would not happen whilst still another thing would happen.

The real rate of interest equilibrating the notional real credit market would not be affected by the 'cheap money' policy: 'cheap money' would not free any real resources. It does no good to supply the wherewithal for would-be purchasers of capital equipment, for example, if the supply of such equipment is not increased at the same time; the supply of resources available for investment can be increased only if savings increase and/or public expenditure decreases. The analogy to the effects of price controls is perfect: if housing rents are controlled below equilibrium levels, less housing will be available; true, more will be demanded, but the demands thus stimulated cannot be made effective. And, in both instances, the price mechanism will be prevented from doing its rationing job, a job that must be done if the economy is to be *efficient* (cf. Chapter 9).

As *liquides* were poured into the economy by officials operating a 'cheap money' policy, powerful inflationary pressures would be engendered; price indexes would begin to shoot up and the current account would crumble. The script seems to have been written for the British economy during the past twenty years or so.

One of the first sectors to get overheated would be *consumer durables*. As the banks became awash with funds, and as inflation-adjusted yields on financial instruments looked less attractive (again note that, when one takes credit, one is reducing one's holdings of financial assets; here it is especially helpful to think in terms of making one's holdings less positive), households would want to shift their portfolios towards durables. To the extent that such durables are traded internationally and sterling was being officially supported, there would be more short-run consequence for the balance of payments than for the British price indexes; there is a mountain of evidence supporting this conclusion. Another sensitive sector is *property*; Mr Heath and Lord Barber will live on forever in economic history; the 1971–75 boom/bust sequence in British property markets, consequent to the expansionary policies of the 1970–74 Tory Administration was monumental. Property—at least land and virtually non-reproducible period houses, etc.—is a perfect object for a speculative blow off: cost-of-production norms do not 'interfere' with spiralling 'values'.

Eventually, a government operating a 'cheap money' policy will own that hyperinflation looms up; it will reluctantly prepare for re-entry into economic reality. Assuming that the liquidity-lake created during the inflation episode is not drained off through the dangerous expedient of open-market sales (risking a financial crisis), stability will be restored when prices become high enough so that the real value of liquid assets is low enough for the public to become satisfied with their portfolios. Then prudent, steady monetary growth, doubtless accompanied by moderate inflation, can proceed.

In addition to the stagnation of the 'real' British economy, brought about by erratic and misguided response by successive governments to the inflation they were making, Britain's real wealth has been impaired by huge foreign-currency-denominated debt, incurred in order to support consumer expenditure stimulated by earlier inflationary policies and in order to support sterling. The latest 'cheap money' episode perhaps has had consequences sufficiently bleak to clear the way for correct reasoning.

4.3.2 The Public Sector Deficit (or Borrowing Requirement), The Financial Surplus of the Private Sector and The Balance of Payments

The argument is based on a simple income-accounting framework. National Product (Y) encompasses Consumption (C), Investment (I), Public Expenditure on real goods and services (G) and Exports (E) and is measured by their sum *less* Imports (J); expenditures on imports do not absorb *domestic* product (hence the British locution Gross Domestic Product). Thus,

$$C + I + G + (E - J) = Y \qquad (4.1)$$

That part of GDP that is not consumed, sent abroad or used for public-sector purposes is said to be *saved* as well as invested:

$$Y - C = S \qquad (4.2)$$

$$S = I + G + (E - J) \qquad (4.3)$$

or

$$(S - I) - G = (E - J) \qquad (4.4)$$

Following convention, we distinguish between household and business savings and classify all investment as business investment:

$$S^a = \text{household saving}$$
$$S^b = \text{business saving}$$

Thus,

$$S^a + (S^b - I) - G = (E - J) \qquad (4.5)$$

Next, distinguish private-sector after-tax income, i.e. *disposable income* (Y^d) from Y, denoting the 'tax take' as T:

$$C + I + G + (E - J) = Y^d + T \qquad (4.6)$$

$$I + (G - T) + (E - J) = S \qquad (4.7)$$

$$S^a + (S^b - I) - (E - J) = (G - T) \qquad (4.8)$$

or

$$S^a + (S^b - I) + (J - E) = (G - T) \qquad (4.9)$$

Putting equation (4.9) into words, the public-sector deficit is *definitionally* equal to the sum of the surpluses of the household and business sectors and the current-account deficit.

Just as the tautology, $MV = PY$, can be infused with scientific meaning only after some stipulations are made about the behaviour of V, equation (4.9) lacks operational content unless quite specific stipulations are made about some of its component parts. Indeed the most damaging criticism that has been lodged against recent attempts by Cambridge economists to convert an equation like equation (4.9) into an hypothesis stresses the lack of empirical support for such efforts; the components of the equation, it is argued, tend to float independently of each other, linked up only by identity itself.

Whatever can be done to equation (4.9) to transform it into an interesting hypothesis, it has great potential as an accounting tool, as a way of organizing data, as a device for succinctly demonstrating the implications of various 'as if' clauses. Thus assume that the private sector financial surplus (deficit)-position is to stay the same:

$$\Delta(G - T) = \Delta(J - E) \qquad (4.10)$$

Equation (4.10) says that, as a matter of definition, once this stipulation is made, the change in the public-sector deficit will be equal to the change in the external deficit! This inference—an inference from a tautological scheme—has conveyed a certain shock of recognition. And, indeed, the exercise permits a nice analysis of the interaction of 'real' with financial phenomena. Equation (4.10) compactly displays how public-sector absorption of additional resources requires, if the private sector is not to cut back its expenditure, that additional imports be sucked in; alternatively, it demonstrates—in a way that seems obvious, once done—that, if the private sector does not increase its financial surplus, available to finance an increased public-sector financial deficit, the latter must be financed from foreign sources (putting aside running down of official foreign-exchange reserves and thus also avoiding some difficult definitional questions); the purchases by foreigners of British securities necessary to finance the current-accounts deficit here turn out also to finance the increment to the public-sector deficit.

Much attention has focused on an enlarged form of equation (4.10), following from the stipulation that the household financial surplus remains roughly constant, but not that of the business sector; readers of the financial press would indeed find it absurd to maintain the assumption that the financial surplus of the business sector is a constant; its massive fluctuations have in recent years evoked a torrent of literature and, indeed, adjustments in Treasury policy. Equation (4.11) follows:

$$\Delta(S^b - I) + \Delta(J - E) = \Delta(G - T) \qquad (4.11)$$

Equation (4.11) was exceptionally interesting in 1974–75 when the business sector was in deficit (at least relative to some non-trivial criteria). The upshot becomes more striking after some rearrangement:

$$\Delta(G - T) + \Delta(I - S^b) = \Delta(J - E) \qquad (4.12)$$

The increase in the current-account deficit generated finance not only for the public-sector deficit's increment but for that of the business sector as well. The British economy was falling into increasing dependence upon external financing; this financing was in essence collateralized by the North Sea oil; the contribution of that oil to future Britons thus was being whittled down. It still is.

Finally, manipulation of equation (4.12) permits deeper insight into the implications of the commitment of the Labour Government in being in Summer 1977, and of the shadow cabinet, to cut back the rate of increase in the public-sector deficit at a time when it is taken for granted that accelerating production of North Sea oil will make the current account much more positive. Consulting the schematic equation (4.13),

$$(1) + X = (2), \qquad (4.13)$$

Component (1) is to be negative, as is to be Component (2). So, using another schematic device,

$$X = (-) - (-) \qquad (4.14)$$

Whether the financial surplus of the business sector (or of the private sector in a restructured formulation) is to increase or decrease is indeterminate *a priori*. The financial surplus of the business sector will increase if the improvement in the current account exceeds the reduction in the public-sector deficit.

The analysis can be promoted by first assuming that there is no change in the PSD and that the current account improves. Then the financial surplus of the business sector would improve unambiguously: to say that the current account improves is to say that less external finance is available; under the stipulations, the accounting identities then demand that the business sector's financial surplus increase. It doubtless now becomes obvious that, as we stipulate a declining PSD, we are *ipso facto* stipulating that the public sector is making less finance available to the business sector. It also will be obvious that, if the public sector were simultaneously to cut back spending and its tax revenues, the improving current-account position would *necessarily* be accompanied by an increasing financial surplus on the part of the private sector.

The analysis so far has developed a script according to which exports increase as oil deposits are exploited while imports increase less, if at all. And the public sector reduces its claims on real resources as well as its tax levy. Households are assumed to consume their tax abatements so to speak. And the business sector, up to this point, is assumed to use such abatements to reduce indebtedness or accumulate liquid assets. So a slack in resource-use has been stipulated. The closure of that slack is what *export-led expansion* is all about.

If we were now to stipulate that the business sector steps up its investment, financing those expenditures indirectly by acquiring finance that otherwise would be required to float the export surplus, we would be envisaging a strongly free-enterprise, i.e. private-sector, tilt to the economy.

If we assumed that households, perhaps encouraged by tax reforms promoting incentives to working and saving, were to increase their financial surplus, the private-sector tilt would become still more pronounced.

If, instead, we assumed that public-sector expenditure growth were sharply cut back, but not tax receipts, and that developing public-sector surpluses were ploughed into industry, then there would emerge an export-led expansion without a private-sector tilt.

Broadly speaking, economic theory is blind to forms of ownership as indeed is, in the broadest sense, capitalist development.

5 Euro-currencies and Extensions

Chapter 5 does not comprise even a précis of the massive euro-currency markets. Instead it explores implications for the analyses of Chapters 2–4 of euro-currency phenomena, especially the euro-dollar. The materials of Chapters 2–4 that are especially closely related to euro-currency theory include (re)disintermediation, 'credit versus money', monetary-base versus interest-rate management-criteria for open-market operations and the slippages between central-bank operations on the monetary base and resulting money-supply effects. Chapter 5 also introduces some new theoretical material, including criteria for appropriate definitions of money-supply in open real-world economies, economies with significant international-trade sectors.

Consider transfers from U.S. dollar deposits to assets denominated in non-dollar units of account, loosely to 'foreign currencies'. True, implications for reserve-loss from such transfers are nil in truly floating regimes. And reserve-loss for such a reason need not be important under the *dirty floating* (of currency exchange rates) we have got. Still *foreign dollar deposits* are substantial. Branches of American banks have incurred many thousands of millions of dollars of euro-dollar deposit-liability. And such deposits can—surely from their owners' viewpoints—be converted into foreign currencies.

Euro-dollar Deposits

A dollar-deposit, received abroad and retaining its dollar-identity, is called a *euro-dollar deposit*.[1] Thus a $1 million cheque drawn against the Bank of New York may be accepted at the, presumptively legally distinct, London branch of the Bank of America as payment for a 90-day dollar-denominated interest-bearing deposit. (Exposition is simpler if a British, French, German, Russian, etc. name is substituted for 'Bank of America'.) Such a transaction has at least two salient aspects.

(1) The euro-dollar deposit is paid for in ordinary U.S. funds. It is improper to say, as many do, that 'money thus has left the U.S. for Lon-

don'. All that has happened is that ownership of $1 million in demand claims against the Bank of New York temporarily has become vested in the Bank of America. The Bank of America will clear its claim against the Bank of New York; the aggregate reserve position of U.S. banks will be unaffected.

(2) If 'Banque de Paris et des Pays Bas' is substituted for 'Bank of America', so that the recipient bank is strictly outside the purview of American monetary authorities, the transaction unambiguously will increase the global total of dollar-denominated deposits. No Federal Reserve credit will be absorbed by the euro-dollar deposit. American banks must charge euro-dollar deposits against their Federal Reserve credit to some extent: the 'Bank of America' case's expansionary effect is qualified.

Relative to *disintermediation* and *re-intermediation,* the best way to dispose of the euro-dollar phenomenon is to classify creation of a euro-dollar as a re-intermediation event and destruction of a euro-dollar as a disintermediation event. To the extent that euro-banks must hold central-bank credit against deposit liabilities, a euro-bank deposit is one within Sector B (cf. Chapter 2). To the extent that euro-banks do not hold central-bank credit against deposit liabilities, they belong to Sector $\bar{B}$. Then, deposit-switches from domestic banks towards euro-banks lead to excess liquidity in the composite sector $B + \bar{B}$, i.e. $B \cup \bar{B}$; the composite sector cannot regain equilibrium until it has expanded its assets. By parity of reasoning, deposit switches from euro-banks lead to contraction in the asset holdings of $B \cup \bar{B}$. Such switches force $\bar{B}$ to liquidate assets in order to pay off depositors. But they do not directly affect B-sector balance sheets. Assets sold by $\bar{B}$ will be paid for with cheques drawn on B^2; the fresh claims against B held by former $\bar{B}$ depositors will be offset by the cheques, drawn by B depositors, indirectly financing the paying-off of $\bar{B}$ depositors.

The adjustment process was disintermediary: aggregate deposit liability was reduced; short-claims against financial intermediaries shrank, the contraction being offset by increased holdings, by the non-financial sector, of longer-dated claims. The adjustment process was initiated by net excess supply of longer assets and excess demand for short claims.

Euro-Dollar Withdrawal and Reserve-Loss; Comparison with U.S Government Withdrawals from the Clearing-Bank System

We now look at 'euro-dollar destruction' from another angle. What if holders of euro-dollars want to hold deposits *not* denominated in dollars? They will sell or redeem their euro-dollar deposits and offer the dollar proceeds for other 'currencies'. Would the aggregate reserves of U.S. banks fall in consequence?

'Yes', under a fixed-rate regime like 'Bretton Woods', collapsed in 1971. With fixed rates, the dollars either would enter official reserves or be presented by foreign officials for conversion into gold, reduction of U.S. swap-based credits (or increase of such debits), etc.—assuming that U.S. payments otherwise are balanced.

Why?

With fixed rates, the 'dollars' would be absorbed by foreign central banks operating to prevent their currencies from piercing their upper 'gold points' *vis-à-vis* the U.S. dollar. Nor would foreign central banks ordinarily use banks in the American private sector; the Federal Reserve Bank of New York is, for the most part, their banker.

Tidying Up the Official-Sector Drain Case

Analysis of fixed-rate regimes has flowed right into that of official-sector drain of clearing-bank reserves. Obviously, events leading to cheques being drawn against clearing banks in favour of the central bank lead 1:1 to reserve-loss for the clearing banks. Switches of U.S. Government deposits from clearing banks to the Federal Reserve comprise such an event, as do tax-payments to the Treasury as they are cleared to the U.S. Government's account with the Federal Reserve. If foreign authorities convert claims against U.S. clearing banks directly into Federal Reserve credit or indirectly (e.g. by buying gold from the U.S. Government) another event draining reserves from the clearing banks will have occurred.

The upshot will depend on central-bank response to reserve-draining events. Thus recall the consequences of a domestic-credit-expansion (DCE) regime: then the monetary authority, sensitized to the current-account of the nation's balance of payments, will alter the growth in the monetary base in counterphase to the trade balance.

Pure Systems of Floating Exchange Rates

To the extent that officials intervene in foreign-exchange markets, problems flowing from conversion of euro-dollar balances into non-dollar-denominated accounts are sucked into 'fixed-rate theory'. Under pure floating, the aggregate reserves of U.S. banks would be unaffected by euro-dollar destruction or creation. Then there would be no official interventions. And unofficial transactors lack access to Federal Reserve credit (again suppressing currency-drain possibilities). No drive-shaft would connect a reserve-creative or reserve-destructive engine to foreign-exchange-market events—unless an impulse were supplied by purposive open-market operations like those controlled by the Open Market Committee of the Federal Reserve System.

Effects of Euro-Currency Markets on Autarchical Controls of Money Supplies and/or Conditions of Credit

In the mid-1950s there developed a heated controversy, occupying thousands of pages and more or less culminating in the *Radcliffe Report* and the magnum opus of Professors Gurley and Shaw,[3] concerning the degree to which central banks could in modern conditions sensitively control relevant monetary/liquidity magnitudes. More recently, the concept of state money, predominant since, roughly, the time of the French Revolution,[4] has begun to erode. Thus the optimal liquid-asset 'mix' of a multinational company—part of a larger choice that also encompasses liability mixes—will include holdings denominated in many units of account. The central-bank credits ultimately supporting world banking systems will, in general, be controlled by as many authorities as there are currencies. The liquidity position of the typical important company cannot be described in terms of monetary *étatisme*. An interesting, albeit somewhat atypical, example is displayed by a Citicorp balance sheet. Citicorp holds thousands of millions of dollars worth of foreign loans denominated in foreign (i.e. local) currencies and based on resources, such as term-deposits, also denominated in local currencies.

The euro-dollar market impinges upon both facets of these dilutions of monetary *étatisme* in quite obvious ways. We have seen that euro-banks belong to the $\bar{B}$ sector in a purely analytical formulation; euro-currency markets promote slippage between central-bank actions and their intended effects on 'nationals' of these banks. And it is easy to eke out a scenario like the following:

The American Federal Reserve contracts the expansion-rate of its credit. Tempered perhaps by some offsetting re-intermediation activity, the upshot will be a reduced rate of expansion of financial-sector liabilities, comprising non-financial-sector liquid assets *and denominated in U.S. dollars.*

Non-American central-banking authorities, except for the German central bank, do not alter the expansion-tracks of their credits.

The German central bank expands the expansion-rate of its credit roughly *pari passu,* absolutely, with the American contraction. So DM-denominated liquid-asset supply can be expected to accelerate roughly 1:1 with the deceleration of the expansion-rate of U.S.

dollar-denominated liquid assets. If elasticities of substitution are substantial, a small increase in the yield of DM paper *relative* to that on U.S. dollar paper will induce incremental substitution of DM for U.S.$ denominated paper; then aggregate liquid-asset holdings of typical companies will expand o'er the world at previous rates, impervious to the Federal Reserve's attempt at contractionary policy.

The scenario points up one of the central conclusions of Chapter 2. Rates of liquid-asset—including, of course, monetary-asset—expansion cannot be directly indicative of relaxation or intensification of pressures on liquid-asset holders. Liquid-asset holdings are selected by portfolio managers; portfolio managers do not react to the holdings they select!

Portfolio managers—decision makers in general—*do* react to changes in interest rates relative to inflation-expectations. Can the hypothetically contractive Federal Reserve impulse be expected to change interest rates—necessarily o'er the world—in ways promoting Federal Reserve plans for the American economy? Rephrasing the question, will demand-prices for American assets thus be pushed down? The answer is keyed to the expected effective cost of borrowing, say, euro-DMs.

German banks will expand their loans and investments at stipulated higher rates. Those planning to borrow DMs and convert them into dollars must consider the exchange-rate-spread component of their effective borrowing costs.

To the extent that borrowers are determined to *cover* their positions by buying DMs forward, the Federal Reserve will have retained control of the cost of borrowing for the purpose of acquiring dollar assets. The discount (premium) on forward marks will decrease (increase) 1:1 with any increase in American, relative to German, interest rates; covered DM borrowing costs will increase in the same proportion as dollar borrowing costs because arbitrageurs will make sure that the forward dollar will become that much more discounted upon U.S. interest rates rising relative to German ones.

Uncovered DM borrowers, if *rational,* will take account of the positive effect on subsequent spot DM prices of repurchases of DMs as debts mature. But they also would take into account effects of differing rates of monetary-base expansion on German and American inflation rates. Inflation in the U.S. might fall relative to that in Germany, thus encouraging increased dollar holdings to be offset by effectively short mark positions. Whatever the upshot, the theory of central-bank policy thus has taken a new direction.

Some Mechanics

Going back to the 'Banque de Paris et des Pays Bas' case, we may build the following plausible scenario:

A $1 million cheque, drawn on the Bank of New York, is paid into BPPB in exchange for an interest-bearing dollar-denominated (i.e. euro-dollar) deposit claim against BPPB.

BPPB in effect draws a sight-draft on BNY in favour of an American company that spends the loan-proceeds with American suppliers.[5]

Now consider effects on:

Global dollar-denominated deposits	+$1 million
Global credit taken (in dollars)	+$1 million
Officially-measured U.S. money supply	nil
Reserves of American banks	nil

The scenario projects a significant loss of control by American authorities over the global supply of claims that could be called 'dollar denominated monetary assets'. The scenario also projects significant dilution of official American influence over credit-emissions to American companies—along lines developed in the (re)disintermediation analyses of Chapter 2. And it becomes apparent that the relevant set of holders and emitters of U.S. dollars goes far beyond the United States. Conversely, how should holdings by say American nationals of foreign-denominated liquid claims be treated in measurements of American money supply? Norwegians surely would find the controlling analyses highly important, more important than the parochial extensions of monetary theory natural to a continental country like the United States.

Concluding Remarks

Chapter 5 can at most merely expand the reader's concept of the boundaries of monetary economics. Perversely, it also has opened up an immense tract of territory that cannot be intimately explored in this book. Only a few hints can be dropped.

(1) To the extent that Americans, Britons, Frenchmen, *et al.* do not operate subordinately to state money, e.g. to the extent that some traders, wherever located, deal indifferently in a number of currencies, money supply 'control' as now conceived by most national authorities, becomes vitiated, even as a concept.

(2) To the extent that the state-money system—dominant only since roughly the time of the French Revolution—does prevail, then euro-dollar impacts—to the extent that these are feasibly measurable—can be offset, in principle, by countervailing open-market operations. Still money-supply-rooted financial policy becomes all the more imprecise: think of the lag in determining what is going on in euro-currency

markets (if one can find out at all!). The context is supplied by disintermediation/re-intermediation theory.

(3) The analysis necessarily blurs money-supply criteria. And it most certainly shows that relevant monetary aggregates cannot be strictly nationally controlled. But, come what may, U.S. officials can dominate formation of short-term interest rates at New York. And U.S. currency will remain the legal tender in the United States; it will remain impossible to contract out of American state money. So the cost of borrowing will be amenable to U.S. official action for a very long time. Inescapably then, euro-currency-rooted analysis promotes financial policies geared to credit-condition, as against money-supply, criteria.

Euro-currency markets pose, in an obvious way, possibilities for evasion of national monetary/financial policies by borrowing or lending abroad. True, costs of covered euro-currency borrowings, intended to be converted into dollars, would reflect higher U.S. rates via the interest parities. But uncovered euro-currency borrowings do contravene national hegemonies, albeit only to limited extents in countries as large as the United States and always subject to the risk of having to buy back euro-currencies when these are strong and the dollar weak (in our particular instance of course).

(4) More cautiously, the implications of euro-currency markets for monetary autarky are not conclusively unfavourable so long as state-money dominates, as it will for a long time. Less guardedly, continued euro-currency-market expansion supplies an opportunity for a more-liberal global financial system as well as an obstacle to *dirigiste* authority.

(5) The closely meshed modern financial network, importantly including the euro-currency markets, leads, especially in small- and medium-sized, highly open economies,[6] to inflationary processes that work themselves out quite differently from the paths described in conventional, mostly American, textbooks.[7]

If say Britain initiates relatively rapid monetary expansion, initial, albeit somewhat lagged, effects will be on its balance of payments rather than on domestic prices. Deficits on current account have been financed for some time in a number of places through government-guaranteed euro-currency borrowings, but, fairly soon—*very* soon under rational-expectations stipulations—the pound would depreciate in FX markets. Costs of imports would go up. Costs and then prices of wage-goods thus would be affected. Trade union wage demands might intensify in the sequel, further feeding illusions that the process was impelled by *cost-push*. Indeed, if British monetary policy were to be persistently relatively expansive, Government after Government might claim, as recent British Governments have claimed, that British inflation was due to exogenous forces causing the pound to depreciate and thus 'importing' inflation.

Pursuing the 'hypothetical' British-inflation scenario, difficulties in precisely plotting the path of future British inflation, together with yield-curve irregularities brought about by Government policy, if not fiat, probably would discourage both real investment activity and domestic savings financing it. Then, along lines recently interestingly explored by Professor Hayek,[8] and deplored by today's *classes dirigeantes,* British lenders and borrowers might try to contract in foreign currencies at rates established in euro-security markets. If they were to succeed, real-investment in Britain would be correspondingly stimulated. The potential of euro-finance markets as a liberalizing force is considerable and ought to be nourished.[9]

6 Share Prices

6.1 Preliminary Remarks

Such consummate masters of the bourse as J. P. Morgan the elder and Bernard Baruch insisted that there was no formula leading to prophesying of share-price movements. Morgan was willing to say no more of the market than that it would fluctuate. Baruch said that there was no analytical key to the market; he claimed to have developed his feel for the market from study of the madness of crowds. The successors to Morgan and Baruch are no less guarded. And academic authorities claim that data generated by share markets support the hypothesis that no predictive formula can be expected to be successful.

But surely the theory of price—a deeply worked facet of economics—can be deployed on something like 'share-price norms'. Indeed, yes: we shall sketch out here a quite interesting Fundamental Principle of Share Valuation. Reverting to the dialectical method of Plato (Socrates), the reader, playing Thrasymachus, might propose the following, plausible enough, strategy:

> One might delve deeply into economic theory. Criteria for share-price norms would emerge. Actual prices will diverge from the norms. So the next step would be to make a short list: recognizing the fragility of the data and the necessary incompleteness of the theory, only major deviations from norms would be further probed; such aspects of a share's characteristic motion as its standard deviation relative to that of market averages and its tendency towards being in or out of phase with the market would be taken into account relative to investor-circumstances, etc. The short list being made, a portfolio (theoretically including some short-sale positions and various option strategies) would be selected. If the selection process were properly based scientifically, it could be expected to be profitable.

There are at least two rubs. How can the theory bottoming such a stock-selection plan be unique: this point provoked *efficient-market* theories of share-price determination. The other rub concerns the quality of data: elaboration of this point provoked *technical analysis*.

It is not enough to 'own' a perfect theory to make money trading stocks. If only one other well-capitalized trader had the same theory and access to the same data as you, 'arbitrage' possibilities would be sharply reduced; if the 'perfech' theory were widely shared, 'arbitrage' profit potential would approach zero. Why should *you* have proprietary rights in a 'perfect' theory? Why should *you* be able to establish hegemony over the market?

As for 'technical' approaches to share-trading, the underlying postulates were modest enough. Assume that you cannot anticipate the market's reaction to 'fundamentals'. Perhaps you would get the data too late; perhaps the data would be cooked; perhaps you cannot expect to contrive a good theory. The response of the technician is to shift attention to a different data space. Ideally, the technician does not care whether the *chart* (of prices over time) depicts IBM or United Brands; the technician works with data generated by share-trading, not by company-activity. The technician believes that he can expect to make money by learning how to divine when a *trend* in a share-price has reversed itself. Again he will make a modest claim. He will not claim clairvoyance; he will not claim to be able to predict when the trend *will* reverse itself; he merely claims to be able to ascertain that it *has* reversed itself. Indeed the *confirmation* criteria used by technicians are highly cautious: one must expect to 'give up', on the average, at least 10 per cent of the 'move'; one cannot expect to recognize the very moment at which trend-reversal is developing.

Roughly speaking, the *efficient-market* hypothesis, embodying rational expectations, grew out of an attack—largely rooted in the universities—on technical analysis of stock-price trends and dubbed the *random-walk* hypothesis.

Common sense impels one to ask the technician how he could expect to make money on the basis of observations available to all. Technicians simply responded by saying that, so long as their theory was not widely accepted, the market would generate appropriately 'patterned' data. Statisticians naturally structured the common-sense-based scepticism more precisely. They focused on *auto-correlation* in series representing changes in share prices. Technicians can be interpreted as saying that such series exhibit non-zero-correlation, that such series are *not* generated by random disturbances. Their critics maintained, and then established that such series could plausibly result from data on random walks.

An effort will be made to translate the thrust of the last paragraph into ordinary English. Randomness is not as obvious a concept as it might seem to be: 'A sample of size n is said to be a *random sample* if it was obtained by a process which gave each possible combination of n items in the population the same chance of being the sample actually drawn' (W. A. Wallis and H. V. Roberts, *Statistics: A New Approach* (Glencoe, Ill.: The Free Press; 1956), p. 115). So the sample that I just have extracted, and then returned to its container, gives *no*, repeat *no*, indication about the next sample I shall select by the same random process. An obvious interpretation of the above example would treat the *population* as the set of stocks available for selection and the *sample* as a particular *n*-stock portfolio. The portfolio (sample) may be selected randomly or it may be selected according to some systematic principle. Various efficient-market hypotheses predict that the latter principle cannot obtain results significantly superior to the former (random) principle. And indeed 'technically' selected portfolios have been tested, and found wanting, along these lines. Another interpretation of the example is somewhat more intricate; additional preparation is required before it can be explicated.

Technical analysis is based on applications of the *conditional-probability* notion. A conditional probability is one that is expressed like this: 'given that Event E has occurred, the probability of F, is so and so; given that Event G has occurred (we assume that 'events' are mutually exclusive) the probability of F is thus and so'. Technicians assert that, if a portfolio-selector, starting afresh today, acquires only stocks that have been in an uptrend and have not flashed trend-reversal signals and then adheres to technical principles over a reach of time (duly noting transactions-costs effects) so that he disposes of stocks that have flashed trend-reversal signals, moving into stocks that are in uptrend or have flashed downtrend-reversal signals, he will outperform randomly-selected portfolios. (Of course, this is but one of many technical propositions and, indeed, is a weak one: technicians traditionally have claimed to be able to beat *all* comers.)

If a technically-based selection-technique cannot beat randomly-based selection, there are at least two explanations. The technical principle may be incorrect. Or there simply may be *no* superior way of selecting stocks technically.

The first explanation cannot be further pursued: impossibility cannot be proved inductively; it cannot be proved that all men are mortal because all men have been mortal.

We are interested only in the *discriminatory* power of technical formulas. Thus, during sustained bull markets, random selection will hit upon more stocks in uptrends than during sustained bear markets. Random selection will conform to technical criteria to different extents in different market phases. But we are interested only in the ability of systematic approaches to selection to discriminate, to improve on 'random' selection.

Moving on to *efficient-market hypotheses and their ramifications*, share-price data generated over an indefinite interval are to be fed into a computer, programmed to determine whether knowledge of what went on over the *x* market days prior to tomorrow will permit selection tomorrow of a portfolio that will yield a higher total return (i.e. accrued dividends plus capital appreciation) than one randomly selected tomorrow. The efficient-market hypothesis holds that the computer always will report back that it cannot find a formula significantly improving upon random selection. There is no need to deploy more technique or words of art than are necessary.

So far only a weak form of the efficient-market hypothesis has been asserted. Indeed a highly inefficient market could generate price movements that would not permit profitable portfolio selection based on study of the entrails: *what if all share prices were at all times the result of random selection of numbers from 'goldfish bowls'?* If such were the case, the market would be both unpredictable and arbitrary, surely unintelligent.

The strong form of the efficient-market hypothesis runs like this:

At any time, share prices reflect optimally intelligent processing of all data that can be known *and* 'shocks' that are equivalent to random drawings: price movements contain systematic parts (predicted correctly by the market) and unsystematic parts (reflecting the random shocks, duly ingested by the market once known). Only the total price-change can be observed. The systematic portions of the price changes will not, of course, be random. But the disturbance (shock) induced portions will be.

To the extent that changes in share prices are anticipated by the market, it is obvious that no trader in the market can expect to gain supernormal profit by buying one stock rather than another stock today. To the extent that price changes are unexpected, nobody can predict them; better, one cannot predict what cannot be anticipated!

To say that markets are efficient is *not* to say that share-price movements are dominated by 'expected' components. It is conceivable that an efficient market instead would be dominated by unforeseeable random shocks. Think of an *équipe* struggling through an untracked wilderness or perhaps of some manned mission to another planet. The mission may command all that is known, etc. But *so* much is unknown. The mission's unfolding experience will be full of unpredictable surprises. The efficiency concept is relative to what can be known relative to the state of the art.

It is useful to supply an example of an expected change in a share-price. Think of an economy that is stationary in real terms but is experiencing *uniform* five per cent per annum inflation. Share prices are expected to increase continuously at a five per cent p.a. rate. Or, anticipating the sequel, think of a company experiencing balanced five per cent p.a. real growth, say in an economy with a macro-rate of inflation of zero. Say that the market has selected a mutiplier (a multiple or p/e ratio) of 15 to be applied to the company's earnings and that this multiple becomes permanent. If the company is earning at the rate of $1 per share on 1 January 1978, so that its share-price is $15, the market expects the share-price to be $15·75 on 1 January 1979. And, incidentally, if the company sustains an earnings-retention ratio of 0·65 so that the initial dividend was $0·35 per share p.a., total return, before tax, from holding this stock over the year beginning 1 January 1978 would be $0·75 in share appreciation plus about $0·26 in dividends = $1·11; the rate of total return would be about 7·4 per cent p.a.

It will be clear that the strong efficient-market hypothesis can be tested only indirectly. Thus imagine that, over a certain interval, the random disturbance (shock) term were *nil*. Then the motion of say the price of shares in Company T, the steady-growth company just considered, would be highly auto-correlated so to speak: far from being random, price-changes from period to period would be perfectly auto-correlated, indeed identical on a ratio scale. The underlying model is contained in a (sealed) black box; all that is revealed to us is the hypothesis asserting that this unknown model is ideal relative to the limitations of human knowledge in an uncertain world (granting that the 'uncertainty' assumption can be seen as a confession of ignorance, recalling Einstein's *mot* about god playing dice with the universe and the quantum theory). The hypothesis implies that systematic selection of share-portfolios will not yield a better expected return than random selection; selective principles would not *discriminate*.

Finally, the efficient-market hypothesis does *not* imply that one portfolio is as good as another for an investor. The efficient-market hypothesis supports the following tactics, and others.

(1) A may be in a low tax bracket and may want to improve his cash flow; B may be in a high tax bracket and awash with liquidity. Crocker National Bank stock, yielding about 6·5 per cent, would appeal more to A than Burroughs stock, yielding about 1·4 per cent; vice versa for B. A will obtain a better score for his *objective function* by buying CKN; B will find it optimal to buy some BGH. A and B are obeying, not beating, the market.

(2) Stocks U and V might be negatively covariant: U tends to go up when V goes down relative to overall Market action. A portfolio containing U *and* V should be less volatile than one containing only U (or U and stocks positively covariant with U) or V (or V and stocks positively covariant with V).

Does the *U-cum-V* strategy sap the efficient-market hypothesis? No. Thus assume that, somehow, profitable arbitrage has opened up between specified wheat at Chicago and at Kansas City. In an inefficient market, such opportunities would be commonplace; even then, oppor-

tunities so overt probably would be part of a continuing process erasing
'cost-unjustified' price-differentials.

Next consider a strategy based on purchase of a 'cocktail' comprised
of wheat and Grain X; their prices are negatively covariant. And assume
that neither price can be predicted from prior prices.

Finally assume that prediction is possible along the lines of technical
analysis.

The three sets of stipulations lead up to some remarks:

(a) The 'arbitrage' profit is equivalent to a pay-off to fundamental
analysis.

(b) The third set of stipulations permits profitable speculation. It leads
to contradiction of the efficient-market hypothesis.

(c) The second set of stipulations permits traders to take out insurance
against risk; to insure usefully but not to speculate profitably.

Pursuing (c), say that you have refreshment concessions at certain out-
door arenas. Your pay-offs hinge on weather and your predispositions
relative to weather. You did win the concession: perhaps you thought
you were more expert at weather forecasting than your rivals and accordingly were able to outbid them. Or, more modestly, you may have
reduced the riskiness of your concession-operations by acquiring the
umbrella concession as well; your demand-price for the two concessions
exceeded that for the one plus the other although your expected post-
franchise-fee profits would be less.

*Efficient markets are consistent with the expectation of successful insurance-
purchase (however indirect) but not with successful speculation.*

An attractive definition of an insurance-action requires that it lead at
best to expected profit as large as if insurance had not been taken out; of
course, an insurance-action reduces variability, and/or 'higher
moments' of the pay-off function.

(3) *Diversification* may consist of buying the stocks of a quite large
number of companies; covariances could be *nil* and diversification still
would reduce expected volatility. The *raison d'être* of diversification in
this simplest of cases is contained in 'The Law of Large Numbers':

The larger the samples, the less will be the variability in the sample
proportions ... If a fair coin is tossed fifty times, the proportion of
heads may well be as little as 0·4 or as much as 0·6. But if the coin is
tossed 5,000 times, the proportion of heads is unlikely to fall outside the
range of 0·48 to 0·52. (W. A. Wallis and H. V. Roberts, *Statistics: A New
Approach* (Glencoe, Ill.: The Free Press; 1956), p. 121).

Diversification is *de rigueur* under efficient-market, and most other,
theories for all but risk-preferers (willing to pay in order to assume
risk!). The expectation that the relative size of any random shock over

the next interval will be no more negative than ε might be held with 0·95 'confidence' if a cocktail of 100 stocks is held; the confidence level might fall to say 0·60 if only five stocks are held; it is easy to convert the cointoss example of Wallis and Roberts to an exemplification of the combined effects of independent random shocks to share prices—stressing the simplest case; insofar as such shocks affect shares generally, they obviously are not independent.

6.2 Economic Policy, Share Prices and the 'Real' Economy[1]

To say, as does the efficient-market hypothesis, that one cannot *profitably* anticipate share-price movements is *not* to say that it is impossible to construct proper theories about how policy actions might affect, *inter alia,* share prices. Take the case of Professor X. X is nonpareil amongst economic theorists, living or dead, in his grasp of the theory of economic policy and its effects, generally and in detail, on financial markets, including share markets. And X gladly owns that he could not expect profitably to speculate on those very effects. Why? By the time X can expect to accumulate and assimilate relevant policy data, X anticipates that the market—including many persons and companies devoting large resources to acquiring and processing data and others well placed to know what policy is going to be—will have done so; X anticipates that the market (seized of X's published work of course) will beat him to the gun. Nor need X embrace efficient-market theory in order to reach so modest a conclusion.

A simple example will secure this new ground. Assume that the members of the market have given expectations about future earnings and dividends of companies that have issued the shares being traded. It suddenly seems to the market that the public sector permanently is to run larger deficits; the earnings/dividends expectations are unchanged and will, here, stay unchanged. Recalling the 'crowding out' analysis of Chapter 2, and assuming that the economy is operating near workably-full employment of resources, the market thus will expect interest rates to rise. Indeed interest rates will rise. Earnings- and dividend-streams will be capitalized at higher rates; present values will fall; the stock market will go *down* (south!). All of this flows from sound economic theory. None of this permits profitable speculation in efficient markets. Nor is the upshot likely to be profitable speculation in sophisticated, albeit inefficient, markets: the exceptionally 'open' American political process precludes privacy, let alone secrecy; successful speculation based on advance Budget information would provoke a constitutional crisis in Britain.

It remains to limn the processes *transmitting* changes in monetary/fiscal policy to the stock markets. We centre on effects on *costs of capital*: the relationship between the cost of capital and its accumulation

lies *so* close to the surface of a slightly expanded analysis.
A few cobwebs should first be cleared away. A clear-headed tyro is
unlikely to be misled; the major confusions about interest rates, inflation expectations and share prices *cum* costs of capital flow from the
hotchpotch of *post hoc* wisdom and 'economic commentary' fed to investors by brokers, investment 'analysts' and, sometimes, the press.

Interest Rates, Inflation Expectations and Share Prices

Prices of shares of heavily-capitalized American companies fell in May
1977. If one relied on what one heard and what was said on the 'Street',
the most authoritative explanation ran like this:

> The Federal Reserve, partly because it was concerned about the effects
> of recent exceptionally high rates of monetary expansion, raised
> federal-fund-rate targets, leading to prime-rate increases on both
> (Friday) May 20 and May 27. 'The Fed bumped up interest rates.' The
> market's inflation-expectations independently increased, leading to
> lower bond prices, although the bond market was sturdier than the
> market for major shares. This exacerbated the downward pressures
> on share prices.

The 'authoritative explanation' is a tissue of confusion. It was
emphasized in Chapter 3 that, while federal funds rate is, from a
mechanical standpoint, an instrument controlled by the Federal
Reserve, the FR must accept stern constraints imposed by economic
logic. Thus, if the economy has approached workably-full resource-
employment (and recall chapter 2's explanation of the likelihood that,
these days, 'workably-full resource-employment' is consistent with
historically high manpower unemployment rates), attempts to push
down funds rate below its 'natural' level simply will accelerate inflation
and inflation-expectations causing the nominal 'natural' rate to shoot
up, etc. Insistence on 'cheap money' would, in such circumstances, lead
to disastrous inflation, indeed to hyperinflation. What actually
happened in May 1977 was that the Federal Reserve, operating its
bizarre mongrel system of money-supply management, found itself
losing control of the money supply: banks were expanding their assets
and liabilities much more rapidly than was consistent with the targeted
inflation rate (rather less than 6 per cent). Subsequent fund-rate increases comprised merely passive Federal Reserve accommodation to
'revealed economic truth'. Increases in other short-term interest rates,
including prime rate (far from a precise indicator of the true cost of
bank borrowing), followed as a matter of course. The structure of interest rates moved closer to (admittedly implicit) equilibrium levels. If
the Federal Reserve had persisted in maintaining a lower funds rate,

equilibrium interest rates would persistently have increased, probably at an accelerating rate; as a result of the FR's prudence, equilibrium rates were lower than they otherwise would have been. The increase in observed interest rates was part of a process that reduced equilibrium rates *pari passu* with the expected inflation-rate; such processes are both common and highly important in correct economic reasoning *and* are hard for most people, including most Presidents of the United States, to grasp.

Why then did share prices fall? It would be stupidly rash to pretend to make an answer. If we were, for expository purposes, to confine ourselves to the nexus formed by interest rates, inflation expectations and share prices, we might suggest that the expected expansion(s) of earnings and dividend lagged behind the actual increases in discount rates. Thus governments apt to follow inflationary policies are apt to act against the *symptoms* provoked by such policies; such governments are apt to turn towards income policies, including dividend-controls.

Conclusion of Section 6.2

It is easy to see that costs of capital are determined in share markets. If monetary/fiscal policy-choices somehow affect capital formation, the share markets either will transmit impulses to the 'real economy' or reflect impulses transmitted by other means (for example, consider effects of official announcements on businessmen's expectations).

A few real-asset market fundamentals ought to be established. It is customary to set up a dichotomy between existing ('old') assets and newly-produced assets. Thus, if the market values the asset-set behind a proposed expansion programme at $10 million whilst its components would cost $15 million in the 'new machinery' market, it would not be undertaken: the project's anticipated rate of return would be less than the cost of capital.

> The price of 'new' assets in the 'machinery' market may be thought of as being determined by production costs and the prices of 'old' assets—including *good will* by the share markets.
> The capital markets, including the share markets, notionally evaluate proposed business-expansion plans: pro-forma analyses are made in which the components of hypothetical plans are treated as if they already were acquired.

We shall probe more deeply into the ways in which investment programmes get evaluated. Then we shall establish the linkage between valuation and economic policy. The criterion dominating management is maximization of the value of a share in the company; in an elementary analysis, it is enough to say that, when a company's balance sheet *cum* activities are optimal, the value of a share in the company will be maximized. We cannot drop the matter so lightly: what if the management disagrees with the market's judgement? Then the management—inevitably challenging the market's *efficiency* in an important sense—might go ahead, betting that, in time, the market will change its mind. The upshot is much too intricate to be further pursued here.

Section 6.3 will study the 'controlling principle of share values' in some depth. All that need be done here is to set up a simple instance that will go to the heart of the *fundamentalist* approach to share valuation while making it easy to see how monetary/fiscal policy can affect this process. The following will do:

Companies A and B both are in steady states; A has been experiencing and will continue to experience steady growth in earnings per share at the rate of 5 per cent p.a.; B's earnings have been and will continue to be 'flat'. B employs a constant amount of capital (we must eschew 'inflation accounting' for now); capital employed per share by A has been growing and will continue to grow at 5 per cent p.a. Both earn 12 per cent p.a. on capital employed. A pays out all of its earnings (after tax of course); B pays out 58·4 per cent of its earnings so that its *retention ratio* is 41·6 per cent. Each currently pays a dividend of $1 per year per share; the B-dividend is in a steady-growth path 'at' 5 per cent p.a.; this means, of course, that the retention ratio is constant.

The market imposes a dividend multiplier of 12 on A-shares and a dividend multiplier of more than 27 on B-shares. *The cost of capital to A and B is the same.*

Next we shall do an economic exegesis of the 'text'. The crucial difference between the operational modes of A and B is that between retention ratios of *nil* (cf. A) and 0·416 (cf. B). B is able profitably to expand its business partially through retained earnings (a channel favoured by U.K. and U.S. tax laws); A is profitable and stagnant; A is rather like General Motors and B like Getty Oil. The financial press itself might write that B's capital-cost is lower than A's. The source of the trouble is the common tendency to forget that a share in a company properly is valued relative to streams running into the indefinite future. In the example, both streams were discounted by the same factor, 0·0833, but the B-stream was *growing*.

We shall not take up discriminatory effects on 'real' economic activities caused by various policies: obviously, an unanticipated policy-lurch favouring the use of coal and opposing breeder reactors will affect stock prices.

Policy effects can be analysed in terms of consequences for expected earnings and dividends and for discount rates. Within this simple scheme, there is something of a perplex: prices of shares of growth companies will be more sensitive to discount-rate changes than those of stagnant companies: the value of a right to $X tomorrow hardly would be affected by even a large change in the discount rate while that of a right to $X in a longer future could be heavily affected even by a quite small change in the rate. And it is the 'future' that discriminates between stagnant and growing streams: the expanding increments in a 'growth' stream become telescoped as the discount rate rises.

Secular policy decisions will influence expected earnings and dividends stream more than will cyclical policies: the streams associated with share-values run over the indefinite future. Still democratic governments tend to sacrifice secular for short-run pay-offs: next year's election is more important to this year's government than the state of the economy in the next generation.

At least since 1965, most of the turbulence in the oscillation of the American macro-economy has resulted from misguided official interventions. This has been true in most Western countries, but not in Germany. The stern West German voters abhor inflation and are relatively insensitive to transient economic events. (But cf. the discussion of *Gästarbeitern* in Chapter 7.)

Inflation-expectations have become vastly important. If interest rates fall because inflation-expectations have eased, share prices probably will rise, but for quite convoluted reasons. If interest rates fall because of an abatement of liquidity preference (cf. Chapters 2 and 7) or because of a permanent decline in the public-sector borrowing-requirement resulting from permanent reductions in public spending in fully-employed economies, share prices will rise for quite simple reasons. If an economy's resources are workably-fully employed and its authorities attempt to push interest rates below 'natural' levels inflation will accelerate and share prices will fall.

A few years ago it would have seemed mad to say that lower money-growth would cause share prices to rise or that higher money-growth would cause them to fall. Not now.

Under more-or-less balanced inflation, profits ought to increase with prices. Why then should share prices go down when more inflation is expected? The market expects high inflation to inflame politics, in turn leading to policies prejudicial to business; intervals of robust real growth, accompanied by moderating inflation, probably will be politically calm so that governments will be freer to pursue economically-rational policies.

Political economy in the West *circa* 1977–78 is in a parlous state. So much so that we need not discuss possibilities of fiscal prudence leading to official policies promoting buoyancy in share markets, thus reducing the cost of capital and inducing privately-propelled accelerated real growth. No short book can afford the luxury of such a chimera.

6.3 Extension of Fundamentaly Based Theories of Share-Price Formation

The reader already will have grasped the 'discounting' idea. So we can concentrate on a few substantive, i.e. *fundamental,* business characteristics that lead to important valuation discriminations between various sorts of stocks. By far the most important of these discriminating characteristics is the underlying long-run growth-rate of dividends and/or earnings per share. This characteristic bottoms the *controlling principle of share-value.* Once the 'controlling principle' is established, a few subsidiary issues can be opened up; we shall examine 'gearing (leverage and share prices', 'earnings cyclicality and volatility and share prices' and, finally, 'dividend-pay-out ratios and share prices'.

The Controlling Principle Valuable serendipity links Sir Roy Harrod's concept of the *warranted rate of growth* of a macro-economy to a correct theory of share-value and especially to the theory of *growth stocks.*

The macro-economic equivalent to rate of return on invested capital is the *capital/output ratio.* Thus consider the capital-stock, K, required to produce real output, y: $K/y = v$, v being the capital/output ratio. The inverse of v, $1/v$, is, of course, y/K. And it is attractive to draw the near-lying analogies between company-profit and y and between either invested capital or equity (depending upon the context) and K.

In the Harrodian model, the economy's propensity to save, s, is defined rather primitively: it is assumed that s measures the constant proportion of y that is not consumed. And, as a matter of definition, real investment will equal savings; product either is consumed or invested. So investment will be equal to sy ; in the Harrodian model, one distinguishes between realized investment, indeed always sy, and intended investment; this distinction is not required in the imitation comprising our company-growth model. Of course, the 'company' model's counterpart to s will be the *retention (of earnings) rate* which we shall call R.

In macro-economies one translates 'investment' into 'change', i.e. increase, in the stock of capital:

$$sy = \Delta K$$

Furthermore,

$$y = K/v$$

so that

$$s/v = \Delta K/K$$

The warranted rate of growth is s/v; if $s = 0 \cdot 1$ and $v = 4$, then the warranted rate is $0 \cdot 025$; then the sustainable real-growth of the economy, relative to its parameters, is $2\frac{1}{2}$ per cent p.a. And, if the model of the economy is stable (economies do not have stability properties;

these belong to modellings of economies), then we shall anticipate that the $2\frac{1}{2}$ per cent 'track' will represent a long-run norm.

It is especially easy to translate the culmination of the Harrodian macro-growth model into 'company model' terms. Excluding sales of fresh stock, stockholders' equity will increase by the amount of retained earnings, i.e. by $R\Pi$. And profit will depend upon the rate of return on equity *cum* equity-capital employed:

$$\Delta K = R\Pi = R\rho K;$$
$$R\rho = \Delta K/K$$

where ρ is the rate of return on equity. The long-run growth-rate of capital employed, earnings and dividends *per share* will be the product of the company's retention rate and its rate of return on equity.

Economists properly will fault our failure to distinguish average from marginal rates of return. If Company C had a high average rate of return *and* expansion opportunities so limited that it profitably could retain only a small part of its earnings, its capital, and earnings, per share would grow very slowly.

Wall Street literature unashamedly blurs the average/marinal distinction. It stresses high rates of return on total capital (high gearing tends to detract from 'earnings-quality', as the *sine qua non* for strong 'per share growth'. Not that this is implausible:

Think of a company as making successive doses of expenditure like the doses of capital-*cum* labour on land in the classical economics of Ricardo *et al.* If capital expenditures normally are large relative to company-profit, so that R is large, average profitability will tend to be supernormal: most of the doses are expected to be supermarginal: if a company persists in heavy expansion, it is likely that such expectations have been fulfilled.

The history of Getty Oil Company up to Summer 1977, and so not very long after the death of Mr J. P. Getty, supplies an important exception to the rule. Getty's substantial per share growth flowed from the company's exceptionally high retention rate juxtaposed with a mediocre average rate of return on equity. Mr Getty had no need for more dividend income! There are other potential forces working in the same direction. Some of these forces flow from biases in tax laws. Others may flow from impulses of managements to increase company-size even if some of the funds ploughed back earn less than the open-market cost of capital.

It remains to transform the pieces of economic logic thus far deployed into the 'controlling principle'. This is easy to do, at least if one centres on *relative,* as against *absolute,* p/e ratios, i.e. multiples. Thus the following rule of thumb easily can be supported mathematically:

Specify a discount rate to be applied to a stream of 'flat' earnings into
the indefinite future. Quite arbitrarily, we shall specify 0·14. Subtract
from 0·14 the inherent growth-rate in the relevant magnitudes
associated with a C share; the 'inherent growth rate' will, of course,
be $R\rho$; if the inherent growth rate were 0·07, and if current C earnings
per share were $1, the controlling principle would call for a C-
multiple of 14·28, for a share-price of $14¼. Etc.

Selection—along the lines of the 'Value Line' long established by Mr
Arnold Bernhardt; this credit *must* be given—becomes 'easy'; what is
hard is to project '$R\rho$' into the long future in a world dominated by uncertainty and containing few precise business figures. One 'should' buy
stocks well below their 'value lines'; one 'should' sell stocks short if they
are well above their 'value lines'.

Coda to the 'Controlling Principle'; What is a 'Growth Stock'?   Most business
growth is *profitless*. Thus consider the massive expansion of the 'fast
food' business, supplying, *inter alia,* junk food. A few fast-food companies have done wonderfully well: long-standing holders of
McDonalds shares enjoy huge paper profits. Many more have folded.
The great majority of survivors eke out a mediocre profit working on
paper-thin sales-margins.

Many unsuccessful investors have confused prospects for rapid sales-
growth with those for earnings and dividends per share. Ideas can be
fixed by contemplating an imaginary industry with a perfectly-elastic
supply curve: product X will, after a short lag, be supplied at $1 per unit
in 1977 prices in indefinite quantity into the indefinite future. This implies that there is a well-defined optimal technique for producing X and
that men *cum* machines can be trundled into place, in the optimal mode,
ad infinitum. Under a *neutral* tax code, X-share holders could expect to do
at least as well freely investing their dividends, equal to all of company-
profits, as they would if X-profits were ploughed back; retained 'X' earnings could pay no more than the implicit charges fixed by the cost of
capital.

The example leads into the characteristics of a 'true' growth stock.
The most-intuitively-appealing sources of per share earnings-growth
are specious in the long run. IBM, for example, has exhausted
economies of long production runs, distribution of fixed costs over
larger annual outputs, etc. as a source of *growth* in per share IBM earnings *except* to the extent that these factors permit IBM to retain more
than half of its earnings on terms superior to those obtainable in the
open capital market. Indeed they do; IBM remains a growth company.

Retention alone can lead to pseudo-growth; 'true' growth is based on
retention that is justifiable under proper capital-cost imputation.
Coda: Profit on Sales and Profit on Capital Employed   The 'bottom line' is

controlled by profit on *capital employed* and/or shareholders' equity. Thus groceries, even when highly profitable, earn very low *profits per unit of sales:* the capital of a grocer is 'turned over' many times during a year. Even unsuccessful jewellers earn high profits on sales: a jeweller may sell only one object a year; he may sell it for $1 million against an acquisition cost of $100,000; he may employ $100 million in capital. The business would be unprofitable if, rationally, charged for imputed capital cost; the rate of profit on sales would be huge.

6.3.1 Gearing (Leverage) and Share Prices

Commonsensical contemplation of real-estate investment better illuminates this space than does the academic literature. The latter, stemming from a classic article by Professors Modigliani and Miller,[2] maintains—with exceptions rooted in market imperfections and tax discriminations—that gearing is irrelevant to stock prices. If one assumes, as they do, that investors can, quite freely, 'make their own leverage', this conclusion easily is reached. Thus assume that corporations (limited companies) A and B are in the same growth-mode and currently are earning 15 per cent on total capital employed. A's balance sheet is debt-free; half of B's capital is borrowed. Say that, *ceteris paribus,* an investor prefers A. *But* he wants leverage; it seems that he cannot get leverage by investing in A shares. This appearance is deceptive: under Modigliani and Miller assumptions he can get leverage simply by borrowing an appropriate amount simultaneously with purchase of A shares. Another investor might, *ceteris paribus,* prefer B shares. But he does not want leverage. He can undo B's leverage by acquiring a cocktail composed of B shares and debt instruments equivalent to B-debt attributable to that number of shares.[3]

Practical men must know that the Modigliani and Miller assumptions about the ability of investors to borrow and lend freely in ways replicating corporate financing are wholly unrealistic. Still they will not go overboard on the importance of gearing in share-selection: much of the risk associated with gearing can be offset in a diversified portfolio; an investor can *roughly* achieve desired overall gearing-ratios through appropriate diversification.

Risk, as logically perceived by the management of Company C, should be sharply distinguished from that borne by a portfolio investor. Prolonged drought is a risk for an umbrella manufacturer and an opportunity for a parasol maker. A portfolio investor can control 'drought' by buying shares of both sorts of companies. And, even if he were strongly averse to risk, he might urge both managements to act in ways exposing them strongly to prolonged drought or to prolonged downpours (a risk for parasol makers); the investor, although risk-averse, will want managements simply to maximize expected profits since he can control *his* risk by deploying diversification strategies. In the upshot, stock selection *does* become sensitive to leverage, although perhaps in ways that traditionally have not been well understood.

Contrast a typical real-estate company with a typical precision-machine-tool manufacturer in certain ways. The former's stock in trade, so to speak, is fungible; the latter's can verge upon being totally illiquid. So a lender, forced to realize on real-estate collateral (as so many recently have done so much), can be much more sanguine than one offering a unique tool-making-machine in the used-machinery market. Two conclusions follow at once:

(1) Considering the *very* negative 'pay-off' attached to *ruin,* the expected profits of the tool company well might become a negative function of further indebtedness at a quite low debt-level.

(2) Since real-estate companies can quite easily float off large debt-issues, relative to their capitals, the indirect cost of borrowing for their shareholders, together with correspondingly indirect credit-limits for shareholders, are relatively favourable.

So tool-company managements will be signalled by the stock market to keep long-term indebtedness under tight rein. And real-estate-company managements will be forced by the market to borrow a lot: asset-rich, highly-liquid real-estate companies quickly get gobbled up by less-fastidious promoters. The *raison d'être* is converse to that supplied by Modigliani and Miller. The nexus in which company (corporate) debt lies is *un*reproducible by investors acting personally; for the most part, the business borrowings of individuals cannot be efficiently arranged directly; individuals for the most part can make business borrowings far more efficiently indirectly than directly, i.e. by buying shares of levered (geared) companies. Real-estate activity is an appropriate source of massive indirect borrowing; tool-making activity is not.

It would seem to follow that returns on equity in typically highly-geared enterprises would be relatively high, at least if capital markets equalized returns to investment at the margin. Obviously, a highly geared company, *earning the same return on total capital* as an ungeared company, would enjoy a higher return on equity than would the latter. In fact the upshot will key into the *demand and supply of leverage (gearing) in the capital markets.*

First assume that there is strong demand by investors for leverage and that supply is inelastic. Companies, real-estate companies, for example, able to supply substantial leverage will find it profitable to employ so much capital that their return on *all* capital employed will fall below the average in the economy; if a 12 per cent p.a. return on total capital, equal to equity, in ungeared companies were normal then companies that were highly geared in equilibrium might normally earn say 10·3 per cent on total capital and 13 per cent on equity.[4] Alternatively, there might be weak demand for leverage; perhaps deductibility of interest payments for income-tax purposes will become constricted. And leverage-supply might become more substantial or more elastic. Then companies would find it impossible to compete for funds profitably unless they could earn as much as the cost of capital in ungeared situations; then a pure Modigliani and Miller analysis would be applicable.

6.3.2 Cyclicality and Volatility of Earnings and Share Prices

A number of hints already have appeared, suggesting that cyclicality and volatility of earnings should have little effect on normal p/e ratios (multiples). The *modus operandi*, again, is *portfolio-diversification*.

Two examples suffice to illustrate the argument. In the first, earnings co-variances are *nil*. The second explores the converse case.

The 'Law of Large Numbers' explains how a portfolio can be more stable than any of its components. Informed common sense develops two other points: (1) variability of share-price, not variability of earnings of underlying companies, is what matters to investors; (2) indefinitely-long dividend-streams, including the liquidating dividend, underlie share-ownership.

Owners of shares in a 'cyclical' company expected, upon purchasing their shares, company-profits, or their growth, to be sensitive to the business cycle: such share prices should not react to experiences within expected bounds. Share-price volatility can result from weak specifications of a company's business situation—ignorance forces weak specification—but not from well-specified fluctuations in, say, 'underlying' profits.

Shares of Company D, whose situation is weakly specified, are to be contrasted with those of E, a company generating profits climbing relentlessly along a gently rising track. Will D shares characteristically sell at a discount (on earnings) relative to E shares? In the first example, assuming a risk-averse world, *yes*. The market would be willing to pay a premium so as to reduce the chance of surprise; E shareholders need not fear what Wall Street calls 'announcements'; a chilling 'announcement' about D could come across the broad tape any time.

The second example is more favourable to D shares. If, for any reason, D is on a seesaw with F, another ill-specified 'situation', a portfolio containing D *and* F shares might be as stable as one comprised only of E-like shares. Proof is easy.

Summarizing Section 6.3.2 the Law of Large Numbers muffles the impact of share-price volatility in any case. To the extent that paths tend to mesh (thus, negative covariance), more-volatile shares may not be discounted at all. In all cases, what matters is not the degree of fluctuation in one or another variable, but the extent to which fluctuations characteristically can be *anticipated*.

6.3.3 Dividend Pay-out Ratios and Share Prices

During the course of a speculative bubble in Wall Street over roughly 1966–early-1970, it often was said, with some truth, that a *growth stock* simply was one that did not pay a cash dividend. The virtuous counterpart to this frivolous misconception stresses that shares properly are compared relative to current and future dividends, that the current-yield statistic cannot properly index what will be the yield-experience of current purchasers. And the 'virtuous counterpart' is amply supported by Table 6.1. Table 6.1 is prepared on the assumption that shares were bought at the highest prices prevailing in 1960 and were held into 1976; the yield-figures show 1976 dividends as a percentage of the 1960 purchase price.

Table 6.1

Stock	Yield on 1960 Price/1976 (%)
Citicorp	9·6
IBM	10·8
Eastman Kodak	16·6
General Motors	7·7
Commonwealth Edison	7·4
Bethlehem Steel	3·7

The first three stocks always have been low-yield stocks in terms of current dividends and share-prices; the latter three always have been high-yield stocks in that context. It becomes obvious that order cannot be imposed upon the discussion unless it is pulled into the field of the Controlling Principle.

Companies under share-market discipline do not retain earnings except to generate dividends more rapidly than can the shareholders if all earnings are paid out. True, in a frictionless world with neutral tax laws all company income would be paid out; then the capital market would claw back the funds, allocating them through a pricing discipline. The dividend-policy perplex has been generated by distorting tax laws in a world full of friction and inertial drag.

Logic demands that there be no systematic relationship between pay-out ratios and p/e ratios *once the influence of other factors is eliminated*. Low pay-out ratios (high retention rates) will not be associated with high p/e ratios (multiples) because the market likes high retention rates; in these instances internal growth of discounted dividend streams based on high earnings-retention will exceed that of dividends reinvested in the open market.

6.4 Additional Comment on Technical Analysis

The premier exposition of technical analysis is contained in a charming book by R. D. Edwards and John Magee, *Technical Analysis of Stock Trends* (Springfield, Mass.: John Magee; 1966), 5th edition. One regrets that the work's signal conclusions have been invalidated scientifically; even our very sketchy exposition of but one pattern, *A Head-and-Shoulders Top*, can be justified only by a 'greater-fool' sort of theory: technical analysis continues to exercise considerable sway; one cannot grip the practice of share-price formation without some glimmering of the style of technical analysis.

Figure 6.1 is patterned after a figure at p. 51 of Edwards and Magee, *op. cit.*, and our exposition of the illustration is but a gloss of Edwards and Magee, p. 50.

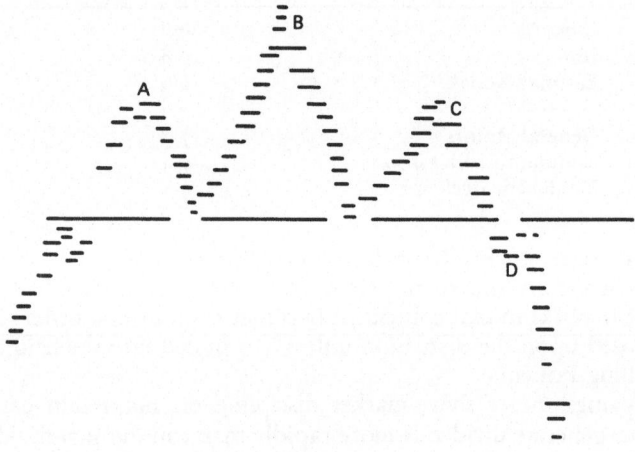

Figure 6.1

The Head-and-Shoulders Top exemplifies a *reversal pattern:* an upward trend is to break down and, after daily prices trace out their strange pattern, a downtrend is to set in. Points A and C define subclimaxes; A and C are apexes of triangular formations that are called *shoulders.* The apex of the central formation, the maximum maximoris of the pattern, is, of course, the peak of a pointy *head.* Point D, or rather Region D, is significant only relative to the 'neckline', 'a line ... drawn across the bottoms of the reactions between the left shoulder and head and right shoulder, respectively, and a close below that line by an amount approximately equivalent to 3 per cent of the stock's market price'. (Edwards and Magee, 1966, p. 50.) D points up the theory's stress on *confirmation*. The adherent of technical analysis must practise stern self-control; he must be prepared to miss say 10 per cent of the 'moves' up and down whilst awaiting confirmation that, indeed, a trend, up or down, has reversed itself. Thus the rally climaxing at A must be on strong volume whilst the completion of the left shoulder should be on declining volume; otherwise the upshot is not truly a left shoulder. Similarly, the rally climaxing at B must be on high volume (of shares traded, relative to a norm, of course). The third rally should be on rather lower volume: the right shoulder concerns an exhausted climber who finally loses his grip. And, as has been explained. the pattern is not deemed complete until the downtrend is quite definitely set in. '*Every* (emphasis supplied) item cited in A, B, C and D is essential to a valid . . . formation' (*Ibid.,* p. 50).

Finally, it should again be stressed that 'technicians' seek shelter from manipulations or, less dramatically, consequences of well-informedness of insiders and others somehow *au fait* of what *really* is going on. Technicians do not seek to dominate the market; rather they seek to react to the market usefully. The efficient-market hypothesis, in stark conflict with the 'technical' hypothesis can, crudely, be perceived as being less paranoid than its counterpart. Or, perhaps better, the former is more sceptical of possibilities of cooperation amidst small exploitative groups intended to consolidate their special advantages (e.g. those flowing from inside information). The efficient-market hypothesis, belonging to a large family of hypotheses supporting the inherent efficiency of open markets and working on roughly the same stipulations as technical analysis, holds instead that knowledge of 'the facts' inevitably will be sufficiently diffused and intelligently processed to assure, through the invisible hand of competition, that prices will not depart from efficient norms. 'The Truth shall make ye free.'

Part II Income

7 Some Income Theory

Neo-classical economists tirelessly have reiterated that, in the long run, growth in output per head depends, by far the most part, on each worker becoming teamed up with more and more capital. An important part of that capital is contained in the worker himself; other sources of productivity-growth are more recondite. Neo-classical economists perceive the major impediments to growth in per capita output to be inadequate or misplaced investment. They blame investment-inadequacy on inedequate profitability: an underlying cause may be discriminatory taxation of business income and dividends; trade unions may be able to push up real wages while impeding productivity. They do *not* ascribe low *marginal efficiency of capital* to deficient aggregate demand. They stress thrift and productivity, the twin engines of economic growth. As for misplaced investment, neo-classical economists emphasize interferences—whether through subsidies or taxes or other discriminations—with the operation of the price system, the allocative mechanism of market economies.

J. M. Keynes's monumental *General Theory* (1936) challenges neo-classical orthodoxy; it argues that the most important barrier to strong growth in mature capitalist economies is the tendency of desired savings to outrun desired capital expenditures if the industrial sector starts to grow rapidly. And Keynes suggested that, most of the time, aggregate demand would be stimulated if money wages increased more rapidly than prices. (One recalls the euphoria over the performance of the Chilean economy in the early days of the Allende presidency.)

The work of Chapter 7 is as follows:

Left- and right-leaning scenarios of slow growth are developed within a loosely-keynesian framework. *Why* might an economy be sluggish despite adequate technological potential?

Liquidity preference is touched upon. Keynes was fascinated by the possibility that interest rates low enough to permit full employment would be barred by cash-preference. Indeed he concocted a phantasy in which the rate of interest was determined by money-supply *cum* liquidity preference while the level of investment expenditure, invariant against the rate of interest, determined income.

The chapter, as it unfolds, gains higher ground. A multi-sectoral model is sketched out; it encompasses economies of less-developed countries (LDCs), the welfare state, international trade, etc. Keynes's central model is seen to be specialized to the industrial sector of a multi-sectoral system.

Slow-Growth Scenarios

Left-Leaning

The marginal propensity to save may be high. Then, as businessmen accelerated outputs in the wake of investment programmes, undesired inventories (stocks) would pile up; lower, feasible, rates of output-growth would be accompanied by excess capacity. Investment programmes would be revised: a low rate of growth would suffice to generate the modest fresh savings required to finance these programmes. Any attempt to expand the industrial sector more rapidly would be infeasible: excess capacity would develop; many projects would be regretted, having proved to be inadequately profitable or unprofitable.

This scenario could be made still more dismal if production-techniques were rigid so that capital-output ratios were inflexible. Then a high propensity to save would require a *more rapid* rate of growth if aggregate demand were not persistently to fall short of supply. But such a scenario, implying no vital role for relative prices so that output-mixes and production-techniques could be adjusted, now would be thought *outré* by most economists.

Under another left-leaning scenario, investment opportunities in new areas of endeavour—think of geographical or technological frontiers—might be shrinking. This would cause the propensity to invest to shrivel up. The propensity to save might be low, but the propensity to invest would be *so* low that even very modest savings flows, generated by expanding GNP, could not be absorbed.

Deepening the Argument

The models of this chapter are over-aggregated, as are most economic models. Thus, in the real world, growing savings flows can be absorbed by a stagnant GNP. Product mixes can become more capital-intensive: think of people buying cars instead of going to concerts, *and* note that seemingly-capital-intensive computers are manufactured, serviced and programmed in labour-intensive ways. Capital might be substituted for labour through *capital deepening*. *Accelerator-effects* might be generated by orders for capital goods incident upon changes in production methods and product mixes.

Demands for investment goods are *derived* from plans to change the scale and mix of 'machine sets'. Such demands result from changes in the planned 'machinery matrix'. Demand for investment goods depends upon *change* in the scale or 'mix' of the machinery matrix.

We now reflect more deeply on properties of an economy with quite stable production techniques, product mixes and savings propensities. Then demand for investment goods will depend on planned output growth, mediated by a quite stable capital-output ratio. The propensity to save is to be stable. So, in the industrial sector of a market economy,

$$sY = v\Delta Y$$
$$\Delta Y/Y = s/v$$

where s = savings propensity, v = capital-output ratio, Y = GNP, and ΔY = change in Y.

Attempts to push forward output at a rate greater than s/v will prove infeasible: finance will not be available. Expansion rates less than s/v will prove infeasible in a more complex way: not enough demand will be generated for consumption goods to absorb planned output; savings leakage from the circular flow of income will exceed infusions supplied by investment expenditure. Nor need the expansion-rate implied by s/v be sufficient to absorb a growing labour force.

It is easy to see how the higher cost of capital, following excess demand for finance, would douse, i.e. damp down, infeasibly high capital-spending plans. Nor is it hard to conjure up a dismal scenario in which entrepreneurial pessimism is self-fulfilling. But will *rational* entrepreneurs who know that an aggregate expansion rate of (s/v) (100) per cent p.a. is feasible, persist in gloomy stagnation?

It is explained later in Chapter 7 that the gloomiest industrial-sector scenario does not imply increasing unemployment. Rather the economy might regress towards the activity-mix of earlier times: the proportions of workers in industrial activities might fall; more workers might go into personal service and subsistence farming. *And* the public sector might expand bloatedly.

Perhaps the most persistent doubt about the political-economic viability of private-enterprise systems concerns their ability to absorb growing labour forces. At least before 'environmentalism' burgeoned, almost all agreed that a high propensity to invest, conjoined with moderate population growth, leading to absorption of growing numbers of workers in the industrial sector at rising wages, would be highly desirable.

Non-keynesians insist that, in a truly free-market economy, unnaturally high unemployment never would persist. Yes, a collapse of entrepreneurial zeal would be regrettable: then wage rates would have to fall or rise more slowly; workers might be released by the industrial sector into personal service and subsistence farming; real wages would have to fall so that more workers could be absorbed in labour-intensive activity; workers might become immiserated. *But* flexible wages and prices would prevent involuntary unemployment.

Still prices and wages are not perfectly flexible! And a socio-political consensus in favour of generous unemployment benefits has developed: in modern welfare states, displaced workers are encouraged to enter the welfare sector.

The public sector can be made into a sponge, absorbing resources that somehow otherwise would be idle. Nobody denies this. Controversy abounds over the query:

Is it sometimes inherently impossible, public-sector absorption aside, for capitalist systems to achieve full employment over lengthy intervals?

The rest of Chapter 7 deeply ponders over the query.

Right-Leaning (Slow-Growth Scenarios)

The socio-political climate may impose rates of profit so meagre that companies will not lightly undertake investment programmes. Making things worse, potential shareholders will offer only modest 'multiples' on dividends: costs of equity capital will be high even if riskless interest rates are low. In such an environment, even optimistic promoters would be deterred by the high cost of equity capital imposed by a timorous stock market.

Fear of expropriation or punitive super-taxes also would depress industry and the Market as would concern about loss of control over management decisions to unions and the Government.

A counterpart problem would arise if tax codes punished savings, either directly or by discriminations against high-savings people. Then the natural rate of interest would be too high for rapid growth; private-sector growth would be inhibited by savings-lack.

Liquidity Preference

What if buoyant private-sector growth would be consistent with interest rates on good corporate bonds of 1 per cent but not much more? Potential bond-buyers would not accept such low returns; risk considered, they would prefer cash. Nor would share prices consistent with so low a discount factor be feasible: the stock market would be frightfully vulnerable to small increases in the discount rate; the present value of a very long-dated stream initially discounted at 1 per cent would be sliced in half if the rate went to 2 per cent.

The Public Sector

High private-sector growth might be preserved by export-sector strength, perhaps bottomed on buoyancy in other countries. Failing that, the public sector is likely to come in. Granted, public expenditure can absorb the labour force *somehow*: e.g., a major war might be initiated by a government worried about domestic unrest. At other times governments might depress the private sector. Such governments are likely 'reluctantly' to offset private-sector 'apathy' by offering 'stimulation'. They will seek to pump up the economy by boosting public spending; the 'crowding out' analysis of Chapter 2 analysed the consequences.

A Case Drawn from an Open Economy with Implications for Public-Sector Analysis

The real, many nation/many economy, world is amendable in some instances to an analysis more favourable in principle to public-sector intervention. An economy may have a dominant export sector: think of agricultural or mineral activity in some less-developed countries. Its low-wage workers may save next to nothing; its capitalists may strongly prefer to save by accumulating liquid assets abroad. A certain equilibrium may transpire: almost nil investment, a strong export surplus paying for capital outflow. If such a country had a growing population, its masses could well be immiserating; there would be justification for diverting the flow of savings, even towards the public sector.

Governments of other LDCs have almost strangled otherwise-thriving agricultural sectors, controlled by entrepreneurs (e.g. kulaks) eager to plough back profits, by diverting resources into public-sector projects or infeasible prestige ventures such as hopelessly uneconomic steel mills.

A Sketch of a Multi-Sectoral Model, Based on Keynes's Theory and Applied to some Policy Problems for LDCs and others

Income theory long has centred on certain esoteric problems. E.g., do industrial systems, *sans* public or subsistence sectors, possess stable 'full employment' equilibria? Correlative quandaries concern properties of 'equilibrium' and 'full employment'. Investors are otherwise engaged; and the prospects of many international companies, e.g. New York banks, depend on the progress of less-developed, sometimes quite primitive economies. Still it would be sad if important hunks of the more insightful parts of income theory would have to be jettisoned in order to build 'practical' models. Happily, this is not so. Although Keynes, for example, was deeply concerned about slumping, mature capitalist economies at a certain time, he built a powerful theory that easily is reinterpreted and refocused so that it can assist probes in many directions.

The Sectors

An economy might contain six sectors, some of which might be empty.

(1) The industrial sector
(2) The pure service sector
(3) The public sector
(4) The inactives sector
(5) The welfare sector
(6) The subsistence sector

Each sector will have special characteristics.

(*1*) *Industrial Sector*   The Industrial Sector is *the* concern of modern income theory, the Public and Welfare Sectors playing supporting roles. In it marketed goods and services are produced by men working with machines. A substantial degree of mechanization is characteristic. Publicly-owned companies like Electricité de France, Crédit Lyonnais, Renault, British Airways *et al.* are in the Industrial Sector.

In the short run, there is little room for increasing employment by increasing labour/capital ratios or switching into more-labour-intensive activities. For one thing, wages and prices are too sticky. So increased employment in the industrial sector depends upon activation of idle machines or emplacement of new ones. Ebbing activity levels in the Industrial Sector would make idle men and machines. The rate at which Industrial Sector employment increases will depend upon the rate at which new machine-sets are put up and on that of industrial-capacity utilization.

Activity mixes are important: are the new machine-sets labour intensive? Also note that changes in activity-mix or introduction of new activities will stimulate investment even if many machines are idle and will remain so.

(*2*) *Pure Service Sector*   The Pure Service Sector contains valets, poets, masseurs, jesters ... Its services are supplied with minimal direct mechanical support. In the Ancient World, the Service Sector was much larger relative to the Industrial Sector than now. Indeed the reader usefully could operate the model on ancient Rome with its bloated Public, Inactives and Welfare Sectors, dominating many subsistence-type economies.

The Pure Service Sector soaks up labour. Imagine an economy containing only Industrial, Pure Service and Subsistence Sectors, shoving the Inactives into a familial limbo. Public Sector Activity? Aside from the odd martial episode, the Public Sector is to be but a stationary drain. Assume that capital-accumulation is sluggish; a growing labour-force cannot be accommodated by the Industrial Sector.

There must be growth in the Subsistence and Pure Service Sectors—unless plague and famine are to 'solve' problems posed by the gross reproduction rate.

(3) *Public Sector* Public Sectors everywhere have, recently, displayed a strong dynamic. Still the Public Sector plays an inferior role in Chapter 7; it is but a catch-all. We already have shown that, as in Nazi Germany, enough work can be made to absorb surplus labour. 'Versailles' can be expanded like a promethean balloon. And, if the terms of trade between 'Versailles' and the Industrial and Service Sectors become onerous enough, violence, such as that which befell Bourbon France, can result.

(4) *Inactives Sector/*(5) *Welfare Sector* What do these sectors *do?* They consume substance produced elsewhere. But how can a child or a pensioner, perhaps eking out a penurious subsistence after many years of service be classed with a welfare case? Economics does not make invidious distinctions: the members of the Welfare and Inactives Sectors do not, as such, produce anything. Economics bleakly asks, 'Who pays?' Inactives pay: parents pay for their children; pensioners draw down annuities. In the Welfare Sector, governments pay. But no functional distinction exists: resources are sucked into both sectors from the Industrial and Pure Service Sectors, together with 'universal' services produced in the Public Sector.

To become unemployed and then either draw down one's savings or receive unemployment compensation from the state is to transfer from, say, the Industrial Sector to the Inactives or Welfare Sector. This interestingly contrasts with counterpart instances in Switzerland, Germany and other countries with numerous 'guest workers', i.e. aliens without permanent residence visas. Upon being released by the Industrial Sector, guest-workers may get shipped out. If stabilization programmes leave untouched the enclaves of citizen-employment while biting into the volume or growth of 'guest' employment, prudent economic policy becomes much more politically feasible. Indeed Switzerland and the Federal Republic of Germany have had excellent inflation-records in recent years.

'Shipped out' perhaps is unfairly pejorative: 'curtailed intake of new guest-workers' is a more soothing, if not lubricious, phrase. And there is natural shrinkage: voluntary repatriation for example. Such shrinkage can be benignly neglected.

(6) *Subsistence Sector* Subsistence-sector members can be imagined simply to grub for tubers with sticks, either in commons or in enclosed

extended-family spaces. External trade can be ignored; trade is minimally important, even within the sector.

A certain snare has engulfed many 'third world' planners. Countries with large Subsistence Sectors optimally would emphasize agricultural development in the Subsistence Sector: it then would evolve into a Market Sector; proceeds from cash crops would finance purchases of more sophisticated goods, including capital equipment, from other sectors. Foreign aid would be similarly employed. Development would stimulate the extrusion of a continuous strand; 'subsistence' families would not be ripped from the land and installed in steel mills.

A Few Scenarios Illustrating the Operation of the Multi-Sectoral Model

Scenario No. 1 plays out in a sub-model containing only Industrial and Subsistence Sectors. Its elaboration roots out the *unemployment* obsession.

The sub-model of Scenario No. 2 contains a Pure Service as well as Industrial and Subsistence Sectors. Its elaboration exhibits serendipity: balance-of-payments theory supplies important analogies.

Scenario No. 3, the *finale*, engages the entire model. There is a collapse of the propensity to invest (in the Industrial Sector of course). It becomes clear that characteristic unemployment effects result from operation of the Welfare Sector, together with wage/price rigidities importantly promoted by minimum-wage legislation. Of course, a family forced to return to the Bush will suffer: the human consequences of slow growth of the industrial sector are not benign.

Scenario No. 1; Sub-Model, Industrial/Subsistence Sectors

The Industrial/Subsistence scenario is easy to develop. The Subsistence Sector does not trade with *anyone*. The sectors are partitioned off from each other except for flows of labour from the Bush and labour-refluxes back into the Bush. Interestingly, the partitioned-off Industrial Sector is conductive to simplistic keynesian income theory.

The model looks like an apotheosis of the 'Reserve Army of the Unemployed' idea. One thinks of a certain view of Brazil's economic development: the labouring masses are said to immiserate in greater numbers in the Industrial Sector instead of their habitats. But surely inherent diligence, intelligence, educatability, submissiveness, deftness, efficacious greed for money . . . are as scarce in Brazil as elsewhere. Surely, all such attributes, responsive to *environment*, will be scarce in the Bush. And these attributes will be of little use to people in the Bush. On the other hand, labour-flows from the Bush into industry will not be at random: the more rapid is industrial development, the greater will be the scarcity values of economical attributes; many workers will significantly benefit from rapid development; their incomes will rise in consequence.

Brazil, no more than the fledgeling United States, has been able to achieve economic growth in isolation. (Maoist China has accepted the trade-offs inherent in choices between more-rapid economic growth and strategic and political freedom of action since its break with Russia.)

Say that wages in an imaginary 'Brazil' are low on a world scale. And it is reasonable to stipulate a high propensity to save out of profits, partly because the rate of profit will be so high. In 'Brazil' a high propensity to save will be linked up with a high propensity to invest; 'Brazil' will be an inherently high-growth economy in just the way that some companies, analysed in Chapter 6, were high-growth companies.

'Brazil' will lack the technology necessary for it to produce many of the new machines needed for increasingly-sophisticated product-mixes. Profits/savings will be ploughed into imports. Exports, paying for imports, will be an indirect investment-activity. 'Brazil', like the fledgeling U.S., will be investing at a rate well above its export capacity: external finance will be required. 'Brazil's' GNP will be less than its national expenditure; the gap will be mirrored by its Balance of Payments deficit, financed by foreign capitalists thus acquiring claims against 'Brazilian' outputs and assets. 'Brazil's' Left will comment on this.

Scenario No. 2; Sub-Model, Industrial/Subsistence/Pure Service Sectors

The Pure Services and Industrial Sectors *trade* goods and services; Scenario No. 2 introduces *terms of trade* within the economy. And, since terms of trade concern *relative prices,* income theory must be integrated with price theory.

If Industrial Sector investment or demand for its exports should falter, the Industrial Sector will shrink or experience a growth recession. Then the IS will release labour or fail to absorb growth in the labour force. Then the Pure Service Sector and the Bush must absorb more labour. It is plausible to assume that the Bush will be a residual claimant: workers will prefer to stay in the market economy; they will seek jobs in the Pure Service Sector.

Accounting for Flows between the Industrial and Pure Service Sectors   Industrial Sector products will be 'exported' to the Service Sector; the IS will purchase PSS services. There will be investment in consumer-durables, including housing, but not in producer's durables, in the PSS; the IS will undertake both kinds of capital formation. So investment activity in the PSS will lead to debits against the PSS's current account with the IS. These debits can be offset by a current-account surplus in other items; or by capital inflow from the IS, comprising a capital-account surplus for the PSS. In the latter (capital inflow) case, claims accumulate in the IS against PSS consumer durables or claims against IS assets accumulated by PSS savers are run down.

Interestingly, the tacit stipulation that payments must continuously be balanced without expansion or contraction of official reserves requires that current-account deficits be offset by excesses of investment over saving. The discrepancies create room for capital-inflow.

Proof. The stipulation that exports (X), like investment (I), are exogenous requires that the sum of the two be equal to that of savings (S) and imports (J).

$$X + I = S = J \qquad (7.1)$$

$$X - J = S - I \text{ or } J - X = I - S \qquad (7.2)$$

Balance-of-payments equilibrium requires that capital inflow (ϕ) equal the trade-deficit, $J - X$; or that capital outflow $(-\phi)$ equal the trade-surplus, $X - J$. Or, permitting ϕ and $X - J$ to be positive or negative,

$$X - J = \phi \qquad (7.3)$$

But $X - J = S - I$:

$$\phi = S - I \qquad (7.4)$$

If the current-account is in surplus, $S - I$ must be positive; there must be capital outflow. If the current-account is in deficit, $S - I$ must be negative; there must be capital inflow. If the current account is in deficit, savings must be less than investment; the excess of investment over savings must be equal to capital inflow. (!)

Sequel to a Slump in the Industrial Sector (IS)

Investment in the IS falls. Or exports from the IS to other countries (not the PSS of course) fall.

There will be release of labour from the IS. And IS demand for PSS services will fall, *at initial prices,* because of the multiplied fall in IS income. The PSS also will feel a cold wind. Yet labour is to be absorbed by the PSS. How?

Prices of pure services are to be captured by a portmanteau variable, P. P is measured by a basket of IS goods: P describes the prices of pure services *relative* to those of 'manufactures'. P must fall! But PSS products are pure labour. So wages must fall *everywhere.* Masseurs might become machine tenders; the IS and PSS labour-forces are highly interchangeable.

Taking up a simple case, the IS, at the outset, is to be in *status quo.* For some reason, labour rushes in from the Bush, offering itself to the PSS. P falls. Demand for pure services in the IS is *unit elastic*: IS money-expenditure on PSS products is constant. The influx will be absorbed.

PSS members in place before the influx from the Bush will be worse off, except to the extent that they buy pure services. Theory is cruel; is this *fair?* If wage rates fell towards zero ($w \to 0$) so that the purchasing power of w *vis-à-vis* 'manufactures' $\to 0$, the IS could greedily absorb an indefinitely large amount of PSS labour. The 'unit elastic' assumption is sufficient (albeit not necessary): as $w \to 0$, labour absorption/IS $\to \infty$; $w \cdot l = k$, where k is a constant amount of expenditure and l labour-absorption.

Any workers displaced from the IS also will be absorbed into the PSS in a free-market system, analogously to the migrants from the Bush. The terms might be very harsh:

> The woman keeps the kitchen, makes tea, Sneezes at evening, poking the peevish gutter.
>
> (T. S. Eliot, *Gerontion*, 1920)

Scenario No. 2 displays regression. An upthrusting capitalist economy staggers into a sort of nineteenth century decrepitude. The product-mix changes drastically. Capitalists will slip into late-nineteenth century elegance: think of the Touchetts and their *éminence grise* Lord Warburton (cf. Henry James, *The Portrait of a Lady*). But there will not be mass involuntary unemployment.

Scenario No. 3; The Whole Model Loosely Explicated

Again let there be a collapse of the propensity to invest. But assume that the Welfare Sector hugs to itself all who can be called *unfairly* disadvantaged. Compassionate legislatures have stipulated minimum wages so high that workers dismissed from the IS will fall into the WS (Welfare Sector): rather than cut grass or wait on table or demean themselves in the PSS, they will enjoy whatever is the largesse of the WS while seeking jobs in the IS they may never find.

The Public Sector (PS) will be in flower. Thus in the U.S. and U.K. for some years now public sector activity, as measured by employment for example, has rapidly grown even when private-sector activity has been declining, by the same employment measure. It can be said that, in many Western economies, 'Versailles' absorbs more than a moiety of resources used. Granted, much of this expenditure is for defence; defence perhaps is the socialism of the classes. Still each slowdown in the private economy leads to countervailing increases in public-sector activity that somehow never ebb, whatever the economic climate.

Under predominant regimes of Compassion, *simpliste* keynesian models are the most practical. A certain Liberal *mélange* prevails: high minimum-wages, generous unemployment benefits, progressive taxation of marginal labour-income in the IS (encouraging evasive action) and tax incentives to 'eleemosynary' activity, together with tax *dis*incentives against such 'unearned' income as dividends. In the resulting socio/political/economic complex, any decay of say the propensity to invest in nations like Britain, France or the U.S. has consequences that bounce about within a rigid sphere, the IS. Liberal Enlightenment has squelched what had been a broad range of 'neo-classical' response in capitalist economies to fluctuations in spending propensities. The response mechanisms deployed in Scenario No. 2 have been knocked out.

Concluding Scenario No. 3: Pulling together Three Strands

(1) Growth *per capita* of measured income, the growth that counts in perceptions of *individual* welfare (Chapter 8 takes up holistic views of society) can be significantly generated only in the IS, at least under our broad definition of the IS; if there is a locomotive of economic history, it almost certainly is in the IS. Still societies such as Athens and Rome ran great races whilst being economically stagnant, even whilst decaying economically over lengthy spans of Glory.

(2) Do not develop a 'right leaning' obsession with the unemployment question. Perhaps it is more *fair* to absorb labour, unable to find employment in the IS, in the WS and PS; perhaps many PSS jobs *are* demeaning.

(3) Paradoxically perhaps, the whole model, controlling Scenario No. 3, has proved easier to analyse than the partial models controlling Scenarios No. 1 and No. 2. The explanation is simple. The WS, the PS and, more complicatedly, the Inactives Sector comprise a Drain: the purchasing power of these sectors is not matched by their productions. This is especially true of the WS and Inactives Sector: past accomplishment of inactives does not change their role *now*. The PS cannot be dismissed so lightly. But the PS has been set up cunningly: those parts of the PS producing marketable commodities have been hived off to the IS; defence, police, etc. are valuable offshoots of the PS but are insensitive to economic stabilization policy and the like.

The Bush (the SS) and the PSS are denatured in an analysis done relative to a Welfare State. One does not go into the Bush when one can collect welfare! And, in Welfare States, wage rates low enough to give the PSS important absorptive capacity would be thought *unfair* and probably would be inferior to WS guarantees: the PSS disintegrates as a focus for dynamical adjustment in a Welfare State.

So, relative to a dominating Welfare State, one ends up on the terrain established by Keynes. However, as was shown in Chapter 2, the postkeynesian burgeoning of the Welfare State has importantly affected weights of emphasis in keynesian theory. Thus unemployment has lost a lot of its sting. It seems much more appropriate now to stress employment rather than unemployment. Be fair: Keynes called his book *The General Theory of Employment* . . .

Concluding Comment

Income theory is surprisingly simple. It also is intractable to moral judgement. What is *fair* is qualitatively different from what is *logical*. But, echoing Plato, is not the True also Beautiful and Just? In a way, yes. And science and aesthetics are linked: cf. the passion for the more beautiful explanation, almost always the more powerful as well. However, Platonic Justice was not what we call Fairness: the music of the spheres is relentlessly exact and carries frugal melodies.

Chapter 8 shows that fairness may become revealed to us but that our own efforts cannot tell us what it is. What is it?

Part III Economics and Ethics

8 Fairness

8.1 Efficiency and Fairness

There may be a sense in which inefficient use of resources is unfair; there is no other sense in which one can *know* what is unfair. It might be *revealed* to you what is fair and unfair; an angel of the Lord may wrestle with you in the night; he may reveal to you what are human rights.

Anticipating Chapter 9, the sense in which inefficiency may be unfair may also be trivial. A group of economic particles, perhaps families, each endowed with a particular set of productive resources. For them to produce the economy's one and only output, a publicly-controlled resource, Econ, must be added; outputs are in some sort of continuous relationship with Econ. A marginal relationship between the supply of Econ to the jth particle and its output can be defined:

$$dx_j/dA_j = f(A_j)$$

Call the rate at which the jth output (x_j) changes with the supply of Econ made available to the jth particle (A_j), i.e. dx_j/dA_j, w_j.

Assume that Econ is distributed arbitrarily in the economy so that its marginal productivity is different for the rth than for the sth particle:

$$w_r \neq w_s$$

If some Econ were switched from s to r, w_s being less than w_r, both particles could enjoy more output if the Econ switch were accompanied by a provision that r should compensate s, as r easily can do: r's output-gain exceeds s's output loss: s can be compensated so that both r and s enjoy more net output than before. Efficiency requires that

$$w_r = w_s$$

for any pair, r, s.

In order to show that the little exercise, typical of orthodox welfare economics, cannot form a basis for social action, some of the stipulations underlying its translation into action need only be sketched. It will become obvious that such stipulations can be valid only as Revelation makes things valid; the climactic revelation will show which revelations are True.

Surely these are among the stipulations required for translation of the exercise into social action:

(1) *More is better than less.* But some of the most monumental doctrinal content of the Christian Church concerns the virtue of poverty, misapprehended by Man, long expelled from Eden. Or consider the virtues of material simplicity urged by such pagans as Mao Tse-Tung.

(2) *Rancour is unacceptable.* The possibility of tastes being interdependent (intertwined) is not *per se* the obstacle: if *r* loves *s*, *r* can make gifts to *s*, up to the point where *s*'s love for *r* makes *s* call a halt. What if *r* hates *s*? Perhaps *r* would prefer having some of his output confiscated and destroyed to being forced to accept an outcome involving any increase in output available to *s*. It may be revealed to you that such a calculus is unacceptably evil. But you cannot *know* that such a calculus is unacceptably evil.

(3) *The living properly can represent the unborn.* There is imbedded in welfare economics, and hence in the theory and ethics of economic policy, a set of deep, and surely unfathomably difficult, problems like those behind Jesuitical pondering on the nature of the immortal soul. In what sense is Jones today Jones tomorrow?[1] The biological entity, called Jones, will not be the same tomorrow. The set of value judgements attributable to Jones tomorrow will be unpredictably different from that attributable to him today. Jones's knowledge of the objective properties of his action space will always be changing: there will be ceaseless extensions, withdrawals, revisions, etc.; the scientific hypotheses appropriate to Jones's actions will be perceived to be different tomorrow in ways unpredictable today. It is not easy to state objectively the sense in which Jones today is Jones tomorrow; something like an immortal soul must be attributed to Jones. So it is not implausible to assert that Jones today is not in any obvious way, even under atomistic or libertarian schemes of value, capable of ordering his actions today so as to generate optimal feasible potentials for Jones tomorrow and tomorrow and ... The State's pretentions in such connections cannot be *known* to be invalid.

Whatever may be said about Jones today and Jones tomorrow, the nexus containing people today and the Unborn cannot be ethically resolved—in ways that can be *known*—by the uninhibited actions of people today. Indeed, traditionally, the State has stood as Guardian for the Unborn.

In order properly to link up the reflections of (3) with the model, we must slightly deepen the model so that decisions on outputs today affect potentials for outputs tomorrow. The upshot follows simply, and remorselessly.

(4) *Holistic conceptions of society are invalid.* (Professor Karl Popper is perhaps the most important of the anti-holists.) In quite recent years, General de Gaulle has been the most articulate, and perhaps the most prominent, of 'holists'. For General de Gaulle, *France* was something very different, and indeed much better, than the *French*. At times, de Gaulle verged upon declaring that he was France—much to the bewildered irritation of the highly pragmatic Franklin Roosevelt. Less exceptionally, de Gaulle stressed that France existed, and indeed lived in some sense, before today's French entered this world and that France would continue after today's French died. Indeed the sacred mission of the officers of the French state—for a Gaulliste as well as for many others—is to assure the continuity of France, whatever may be the faults of Frenchmen.

Holism is not confined to matters of politics and government. Consider *culture*. Thus Bertrand Russell and other advocates, some years back, of unilateral nuclear disarmament deemed the transmission of the culture to be lexicographically predominant. The *culture*—presumably the music of Bach and Mozart, the painting of Leonardo and Cézanne, the poetry of Shakespeare, etc.—of Western Man, for example, means something different from the cultural achievements and attitudes of men in the West. One may assert this. One cannot be *proved* to be wrong. It may be revealed to you that another thus is wrong. It may be revealed to him that he is not.

Again turning to the little model, it is at least heuristically appealing to assume that, under an efficient distribution of the Resource, so that no economic particle could achieve a position more preferred *by it* unless at least one other particle thus would have to accept a position less preferred *by it* (cf. the brief discussion of optimality in the sense of Pareto in Chapter 9), the music of Mozart, the poetry of Baudelaire, etc. would fade away whilst, under some inefficient Resource allocations, culture would thrive. I may then prefer an inefficient allocation. As the head of the state and its government, I may implement this preference. You may be of another mind. One cannot *know* who is right. One cannot *know* whether the first or the second or the . . . regime is fair.

Chapter 8 will somewhat deepen and expand these reflections. It is important, in any case, not to be ensnared by nihilistic temptations that might flow from the analysis. To say that the Right Action cannot be inferred from objective premises in the manner of science is not to say that any action is as ethically proper as any other action. Nor does the analysis deny that we can convince each other about the nature of the Right Action; indeed the Platonic–Aristotelian–Thomist tradition centres on inference of the Right Action from premises that in general cannot be 'known' but which instead become stipulated by ethical conviction, rooted in Revelation. *The analysis does militate against translating confusion between revealed and objective stipulations into arbitrary, pseudo-scientific prescriptions for social action.* Chapter 9 will clarify any remaining difficulties: it will become clear that, in vast reaches of the domain of economic policy, correct inferences about efficient and inefficient economic states will generate consensus about what is the Right Action. It is no minor thing to be able to infer from premises, whatever their teleological origins, what are (admittedly relatively) optimal actions.

8.2 Morality and Amorality in Affairs of State; Remarks on the Law of the Constitution

If this book were a treatise—indeed it is not!—this chapter would supply at least a précis of the history and current state of welfare economics. As it is, we have made straight off somewhat fragmented, and surely sceptical, remarks about the intersection of social theory and objective, as against revelatory, regions of knowledge of the Right Action.

Man does not live by bread alone. The theory of political obligation, containing the law of the constitution, is a better starting point than, for example, the query: 'can one deduce that distribution of material wealth that is the most fair?' (No!)

We begin shockingly: law is not justice (!).

In Austinian jurisprudential theory, it is possible to eke out the set of decision rules, comprising 'the law', like this:

Consider the set of fact situations, F, that can give rise to consequence in law. Each element in F yields a set of rights, duties, powers, liabilities, etc. determined by the ancient common law, for example, and so controlled by a body of case-law, following *stare decisis,* of almost immemorial antiquity. The legal process maps F into the set of decisions, D: 'You shall pay £1,000 damages to Doe'; 'You are entitled to a cease-and-desist order against Roe'. The decision-process, f, is stochastic; it cannot be predicted with perfect confidence what 'point' in D will be associated with some 'point' in F. Law-study is concerned with the properties of f; weighty scholars strenuously disagree about what these are.

There is a proper, and an improper, sense in which one can say that 'the law', f in F, *should* be thus and so.

Consider the law of the American Constitution. I find it incomprehensible that it could seriously be said that the death penalty is unconstitutional. The death penalty was quite often meted out in, I think, all the states represented in the 1787 Convention or the subsequent ratification process. No subsequent amendment can be construed, under the canons of constitutional construction, as barring the death penalty. So there is a proper sense in which one can say that the law *should* be thus and so.

Another might say, 'the death penalty is a barbaric relic of past times; it ought to be abolished in case law; it *should* be found unconstitutional'. This is a highly improper statement. For courts to map from F to D guided by what they think has been revealed to them by God or by what they are sure is *fair,* rather than by the positively, if not easily, known f, is for law to be abolished too.

Is the death penalty unjust? Is it fair? I do not *know. I cannot know.* The President in Congress, the various governors, in the various state legislatures, might say that the laws they make or repeal or veto are just or unjust. I cannot *know* what they mean.

To repeat, to say that notions of justice or fairness are beyond the ken of legal or economic science is not to say that whatever it is that 'morality' is simply is unimportant. It only is to say that such concepts are *au dehors* of *science.*[2]

Moving on to morality and amorality in affairs of state generally, one almost inevitably recalls perhaps the most famous of all collisions between morality and amorality in foreign affairs, that between Caesar and God.

Pilate therefore said unto him, Art thou a king then? Jesus answered, Thou sayest that I am a king. To this end have I been born, and to this end am I come into the world, that I should bear witness unto the truth. Every one that is of the truth heareth my voice. Pilate saith unto him, What is truth? (St. John 18)

I [Pilate] will therefore ... release him. But they cried out all together, saying, Away with this man, and release unto us Barabbas ... They shouted, saying, Crucify, crucify him. And he said ... I ... will release him. But they were instant with loud voices, asking that he might be crucified. And their voices prevailed. And Pilate gave sentence that what they asked for should be done ... Jesus he delivered up to their will. (St. Luke 23)

Pilate could not *know* what was Truth. The lamentable consequence of his passivity often has been cited as proof of the need for judges to consult God as well as f. But Jesus does not support such an inference: 'Every one that is of truth heareth my voice'. Am I of truth? Have I heard his voice? Have you? What is truth? Law cannot be founded upon what cannot be *known.*

Jeanne d'Arc heard voices. She answered them. She killed Englishmen. Others have heard other voices. Your voices may tell you that she was right, or wrong. Still voices cannot lead to a Rule of Law.

Pilate the judge was subordinate to Pilate the Roman. Pilate consulted Rome's interests in the sense of what now often are called *Metter-nichian* interests. Are there higher terms of reference that Pilate *should* have consulted? I cannot *know* what he should have done. Moral imperatives must be *revealed* to me; moral imperatives transcend analytical reasoning; alternatively they have no objective meaning.

In 1977 the United States has a President who hears voices. President Carter appears to be more plangently the receptacle of the divine will than has been any President since Woodrow Wilson. *Human rights* are said in 1977 to be part of the foundation of American foreign policy.

Before the United States became a powerful nation, its diplomacy was a model of *Realpolitik*. Washington denounced the French treaty. John Adams was forced into a sort of war with France but did not blunder into a war with Britain, even though he hated Hamilton. Hamilton was in league with the British: he leaked the highest secrets of the American state to the British ambassador. Daniel Webster practised a different sort of *Realpolitik*: he solicited cash bribes from the British while serving as American Secretary of State. Theodore Roosevelt, at the dawn of American power, 'took Panama'. Indeed the origins of Manifest Destiny in American foreign policy are imperialistic. America's 'winning streak' was broken in Vietnam. The dismal upshot shows again that wars fought under the logic of national interest are apt to be more restrained, and much less frequent, than wars undertaken for 'human rights' or some other purpose that cannot be *known*.

8.3 From Hobbes to Freud; Remarks on Superego Formation as a *Sine Qua Non* for Cooperative Action

To say that the intersection of economics and ethics is empty is not to say that conscience or ethical sensitivity is immaterial to the success, indeed the survival, of societies.

In the beginning, as described in Hobbesian pseudo-history, man was in an id regime. There was no possibility for cooperative social action in life, doubtless blessedly short as well as brutish. The id regime, lacking cooperation, is pre-economic, pre-societal.

The *ego principle* leads up to organized society. One recalls an infant in Freudian literature. He thrashes about, touching a hot stove. Thus *id*. He becomes aware of pleasure/pain; cf. the hedonistic calculus of economics. He establishes a sense of self *vis-à-vis* an exterior (the 'world'); this leads up to an optimizing calculus, again stressing how the *ego-principle* links up with economic theory. Next there is the *superego principle*. The infant is taught not to make a great to-do if burnt or that there is a *taboo* against touching hot stoves. There may be counterpart *totem* ideas: recall the historic link between epilepsy and prophecy, indeed revelation.

The ego-principle promotes *possessive individualism.* Welfare economics comprises an elegant elaboration of the effects of interaction of possessive individualism with ego-based cooperative mechanisms such as factories, markets and joint ventures.

Cooperation basically is anti-id; in modern economics it is a supreme fulfilment of the ego-principle. Still economic/social cooperation must be bolstered by superego elements: the ego-principle is consistent with murder, vandalism and theft in business competition, with ruthless disdain for consumer-health, etc. Indeed, short of shared commitment over a wide range of affairs, state sanctions would be insufficient to establish the behavioural restraints vital for organized society.

So 'liberalism' is an insipid, if not poisoned, chalice. The atomistic model of possessive individualism, *cum* liberal doctrine (always in the traditional European sense of that word) cannot adequately explain the structure of a modern society; it is unable to explain vital superegoistic content. *Au fond,* economic man tacitly possesses characteristics not at all evident in the mathematics of utility theory. 'Economic man's *tastes,* rarely dilated upon in economic theory, are the consequence of certain sorts of upbringings and experiences. Think of urban man. He must needs think of himself as totally dependent upon the restraint, if not the goodwill of his fellows: otherwise the risks of crossing the street in heavy traffic would be profound; more sentimentally, perhaps, Everyman would shrivel up and die if deprived, always, of the smiles of those he might encounter. More to the point, perhaps, in a basically economic discourse, Everyman, city-dweller, finds public goods bulking *so* large in his consumption: streets, sewers, water-supply, police-protection (*useless* unless the citizenry basically is law-abiding), parks and, to repeat, the sense of community.

The ego-principle orientation of 'liberal' doctrine is indeed striking. The standard models of general economic equilibrium might be said to lack gravitational principles: the economic particles are deemed to be psychologically and sociologically independent, arriving at cooperative arrangements in order to increase individual real wealth and, indeed, in general competitive equilibrium achieving an *efficient* resource-use. In the life of a real society, containing an economy of course, there must be a strong superego orientation: otherwise such concepts as sacrifice, compassion, affection for strangers, etc.—all fundamentally important to what we call civilized life—would depend upon ultimate rationalizations of citizens possessed of supreme self-control, the kind of citizens that do not and never will exist. And, to repeat, the state is supreme in the domain of the superego principle: the state is the custodian of group conscience and of the continuity of social and cultural institutions. The transition from Hobbes's notional pre-political Horror to a modern Western state is nothing more than the history of the expansion of the field controlled by the superego principle.

8.3.1 Extension of Section 8.3 to the Question of Equality: Is Inequality Fair?

Consciousness of inequality as an ethical problem flows from particular superego formations. Highly civilized, indeed brilliant, societies such as those of ancient Greece and Rome regarded inequality in all of its dimensions as a natural condition, perhaps to be explained but not requiring justification. Admittedly the Christian Church has an am- biguous position: the early Christians stressed the virtues of poverty as a preparation for entrance into afterlife; Calvinism borrows heavily from the Old Testament, describing how Israelites favoured by Yahveh (usually because of qualities of blind obedience and unlimited sufferance) came to possess waxing flocks and fertile women. In any case the exceptional sensitivity to the ethical connotations of material in- equality that characterizes modern Britain (and also the Nordic democracies for example), like the growing concern, expressed in Poor Law debates and in many sincere, if misguided, protestations about the consequences of industrialization, as the nineteenth century went on and culminating in the welfare legislation of the Campbell-Bannerman and Asquith Administrations (including Lloyd George and Churchill of course), obviously is rooted superegoistically. Nor should one ignore the powerful and quite spontaneous eleemosynary forces that have developed in private sectors of say Britain and the United States right through periods that have been called *laissez-faire*. Indeed it can be argued that the present British welfare state has, to the extent that its tax laws punish philanthropy for example, forced much substitution of public for private welfare-impulse.

It is not surprising then that economists, especially in Britain and America, have written much about (in)equality. Perhaps it is surprising that what they have written on that subject has virtually no valid content.

In a way, economists stumbled upon 'scientific' treatment of the ethics of (in)equality both needlessly and accidentally. Thus at one time it was thought that scientific treatment of the theory of demand required the notion of *utility,* itself at least implicit in the writings of Jeremy Bentham on the hedonistic calculus (although marginal-utility theory's foundations mostly were established by Austrian writers). It has turned out that neither the pure theory of demand nor econometric work in consumption, marketing, etc. requires the *utility* notion: indeed *utility* must be dropped if economic theory is to achieve its most generalized form. So indeed *utility* was a needless 'discovery'.

Economists, pursuing utility theory, *accidentally* stumbled into the 'fairness' thicket in the following way. In order to get the curvature properties (of the *utility function*) that they thought they required (for convexity properties), and simply because it seemed 'obvious' that such was the case, they (for the most part needlessly) assumed that the marginal utility of wealth (called 'income' in the literature) diminished as wealth increased. They at least tacitly assumed that 'utility' could be

cardinally measured and that the metric was commmon to all 'consumers'; both of these assumptions are fatuously otiose for a rigorous
demand theory. All of this having happened, utility theory got absorbed
into efficiency analysis or, better, mixed up with efficiency analysis: if, in
such a mode of analysis, national utility (sometimes called the 'greatest
good of the greatest number') were to be maximized and if—in some
sense defying sophisticated analysis—all consumers were alike (here we
see the desideratum *equality* overwhelming the structure of the theory so
that the assumption that all are equal as 'utility generators' forces the
conclusion that wealth should be equally distributed; cf. *infra*), then
wealth would have to be equally distributed since only then could the
necesssary condition for efficiency

$$U_r = U_s \qquad (U_i = \mathrm{d}(\mathrm{f}'W))/\mathrm{d}W_i)$$

be met.

More recently, an intellectually more reputable, albeit empirically in-
operable, argument has taken hold. A distribution is said to be unfair if
Jones and Brown both prefer Jones's position. According to this argument, redistribution should persist until Brown no longer prefers
Jones's position while Jones continues to prefer his position to Brown's;
and, of course, this should hold for any pair. These criteria might be
called an apotheosis of Envy.

Little comment is necessary. The model implicit in the 'theory' might
be pertinent to a group of victims of a shipwreck doomed to eternal
exile on a remote island otherwise uninhabited. It cannot be operated
for an advanced economy; in an advanced economy each member's
position at each instant changes: my endowment changes as a consequence of my actions over, say, the day concluded at this instant
relative to shifts eternally occurring in what is for me my environment
and I am in continual biological transition (culminating in death). Does
Jones's child 'belong' to him? Should we ignore the cultural consequences of Jones, instead of Brown, being rich? A wealthy Jones
would be a patron of chamber music; a wealthy Brown would build
some folly. Economists have no expertise on fairness. Does anyone? No.
It can be revealed, but it cannot be known, what is fair.

Economics *can* promote the socio-political consensus so important to
a successful state. If a much-more-equal distribution of wealth were
shown to cut back the growth-rate of national income from 4 per cent to
say ½ per cent, 'reform' might be universally rejected: it might become
agreed that such a 'reform' would injure, not help, the poor. Is it Good
that young men should do social work instead of entering business in
order to make money? Economics might show that the acquisitive
choice usually leads to wealth-creation exceeding *richesses* flowing back
to the putative entrepreneurs; and that anti-materialistic Alyoshas
typically become middle-aged parasites, consuming product that might
flow into capital-formation, benefiting the complementary factor,

labour. A consensus less averse to acquisitiveness might emerge quite spontaneously.

8.3.2 Extension of Section 8.3 to Conservation: Petroleum; Remarks on O.P.E.C.

'Conservation' is a transitional topic. On its surface, the gist of the matter would seem to concern efficiency—hence Chapter 9. But, when the matter is probed more deeply, the controlling material centres on certain essential differences between 'commercial' and 'social (or *étatiste*) discounting.

Will a free-market system adopt appropriate practices concerning petroleum (hereafter *oil*) reserves relative to exploration potential?

Relative to the 'egoistic' criteria governing the interest-rate structure of a competitive capitalist system: *yes*.

Relative to the 'superegoistic' criteria that lead up to the programme of action of a government, so to speak the operational branch of the State: in general, *no*.

Go back to the notion of *present value* developed in Chapter 6. Assume that the earnings of a typical company (corporation) are discounted at a 10 per cent rate; the tax-adjusted cost of capital then will be 10 per cent. A tacit market in oil futures will develop. The shadow, if not the actual, price of oil for delivery say five years from now will bear a normal relation to the price of spot oil. There will be a normal *backwardation*. Interest and storage costs (doubtless slight for oil in the ground) will determine the premium enjoyed by future over spot oil; interest rates readily can be recast as discount rates.

Say that there develops a growing awareness that, at current rates of extraction, world oil reserves will decline so that a crisis will ensue by 1990. Along lines developed for markets for currency-futures in Chapter 5, future-oil prices would shoot up, dragging up the price of spot oil in line with the formula tacit in the last paragraph. Conservation thus would be encouraged, as would exploration. The Market cannot properly be said to be predominantly myopic.

Reflect on *discounting*. The present value in 1977 or 1978 of 1990 receipts will, of course, be very substantially less than their nominal value. So a certain impatience becomes imparted to free markets, quite rationally. Rational calculation of profit-, or utility-maximizers, pursuing ego-principle-dominated strategies, discounts the future.

Next put into play a notional population-class, *the unborn*, represented by the State, the Guardian of Continuity. The Minister of State for the Unborn correctly will discount *backwards* so to speak. He would hope that the Living, for whatever reason, become abstemious so that resources become conserved and current product flow into capital for-

mation, etc. In brief, the minister would, in his parochial capacity, seek
not to maximize present values but rather, in an admittedly imprecise
sense, to maximize endowments at what might be remotely future dates.

So a certain intertemporal tussle is inherent in any society's decision-
making processes. Nor would a modern society be viable if superegoistic
impulses were not prominently active in resolving the inherent conflict
between the Born and the Unborn. It would be quite normal for an aged
person with no family at all to be deeply concerned about the condition
of wellbeing, and the state of the arts, in his country, if not in the world,
long after he is dead. In the upshot political processes in the broadly
consensual societies of the West have been able to resolve this intertemporal tussle fairly easily; the admittedly precarious political/economic
future of many of these societies more reflects the radiated influence of
longstanding academic hostility towards capitalism than inherent,
mechanical failures of the capitalistic economies, nested in political
systems in which the State acts as Guardian of Continuity, we have had.
Not for the first time is the order of things threatened by a *trahison des
clercs*.

It is impossible to reduce the implications of the analysis to a set of
formulas or even to some well defined paradigms. The crucial choices
are not even in the domain of economics. It is possible to say this much.

(1) Once we make the obvious extension of superegoistic considerations
to the future and thus to the Unborn, and to the continuity of the arts
and of the society, the State as Guardian of Continuity inevitably and
properly will upset some of the results generated in free markets—essentially controlled by the ego-principle. Admittedly these interventions
always seem to be clumsy and often are counterproductive.

(2) 'Conservation' is not unambiguously in the service of the Future.
Thus 'environmentalist' pressures in the United States have for some
years both impeded extraction and transportation of 'new' crude oil
from such places as Alaska *and* growth of nuclear-based energy-source
alternatives to oil. At the same time Britain opted for rapid exploitation
of its North Sea oil-deposits. As a result, by mid-1977 the British state
could anticipate virtual energy autarky (qualifications are rooted in persistent disappointments in what had been a most promising nuclear-
energy prospect) while America was frustratedly groping about, having
realized that its strategic posture had become seriously weakened by
dependence on external energy-sources. The American state and its
security (and hence continuity) had been damaged by 'conservation' just
as the British state had been strengthened by what some called at the
time an anti-conservationist programme.

There is a tendency to underestimate innovative potentials in resource
discovery and substitution. Clearly the society's future would better be
served by a more-rapid exploitation of its initially seemingly relevant

resources, leading to a more-massive accumulation of capital, followed by developments opening up hitherto neglected, but abundant, resource deposits than by stern conservation of the initial 'operational' set of resources leading up to diminished capital accumulation and inability to exploit neglected deposits.

Still, *en principe,* the Market is *not* an infallible guide for conservation-practice; the Market does not, in its nature, fully respond to superegoistic based factors.

(3) One reason why the upshot is so cloudy is that, after all, we cannot predict what will be our new knowledge and, of course, the consequences of that knowledge. Economic policy is less than guesswork; there is no point in trying to predict the unpredictable; trend-extrapolation, fragile as it is, is most of what we have got. Underlying much modern analysis of economic policy is the recognition that economic theory crumbles as it is examined more closely. The longer one studies economic theory, the less one is apt to be willing to conclude from it.

Remarks on O.P.E.C. The massive increase in the oil price since late 1973, at the least encouraged (!) by O.P.E.C., seems unfair to some: why should Arabia, for example, now be so rich when it has not, in the ordinary sense, *earned* its immense wealth? But why is the reader, if he is not a citizen of Bangladesh, so much richer than such a citizen? He does not deserve to be as rich as that; the other does not deserve to be so poor. What is Fair? One cannot *know* what is fair.

Confining ourselves to objective aspects of the O.P.E.C. regime, two subjects will briefly be studied: 'recycling' of 'oil' dollars; 'is O.P.E.C. a cartel?'

Recycling O.P.E.C. powers enjoying the largest balance-of-payments surpluses tend to have a low capacity to absorb imports and tend to be financially highly conservative.[3] Import-absorptive capacity can be put aside: this helps explain why Saudi Arabia for example runs such large surpluses. The financial conservatism of such countries as Saudi Arabia has led to certain effects closely related to the analysis of Chapter 2. Thus cautious savers generally do not invest directly in risky ventures. Instead they make placements with financial institutions; at least at some time during 1975–76, 10 per cent of Citibank's deposits were placed by Kuwait; vast deposit-inflows were received by selected, always massive, banks such as Chase Manhattan, Citicorp and Morgan. Most of these were euro-currency deposits; predominantly, euro-dollar deposits. And, willy-nilly, the banks, as they lent out (invested) these fresh 'resources', *recycled petro-dollars.* Petro-dollars? Petro-dollars are *not* analogous to euro-dollars: they simply are, in the aggregate, the sum of balance of payments deficits on oil-account; petro-dollars have no operational meaning; they simply are a figure of speech.

There has been much confusion, partly because of misplaced efforts by some bankers to establish their 'social responsibility', about the role of the banks in the recycling process. Thus it is widely believed that the banks mostly have 're-lent' the petro-dollars directly to public authorities bridging balance-of-payments deficits, including 'poor, non-oil' countries. No, the banks have not been making significant loans to 'poor, non-oil' countries. The other notion is half-true, although the untrue half is the more interesting.

Balance-of-payment-deficit financing by big banks indeed has occurred, and has bulked larger, in recent years; a sceptical précis of this development was made in Chapter 2. Much the greater part of bank lending associated with recycling of petro-dollars has been for project-finance; this lending has, at least in an *ex post* sense, bridged 'oil' deficits, especially of medium-income, fast-growing, non-oil, less developed countries (LDCs), but only indirectly. Thus consider non-local-currency components (again cf. Chapter 2) of lending to entities based on Brazil, Mexico (an important oil producer), Korea, Formosa, Argentina (*not* a rapidly growing economy) *et al.* Reduce the compass of the analysis further: i.e. to the confines of euro-currency lending supported by petro-dollar inflows into banks. The context of the project loans simply concerns ordinary project, i.e. commercial and industrial (C & I) financing, relative to country risk. True, bankers will be aware that, *ceteris paribus,* their lending represents an inflow of say dollars into the borrower's country. But usually the dollar proceeds are to be spent abroad; if the transaction merely covered a governmental effort to increase foreign-currency reserves (cf. the references in Chapter 5 to Electricité de France, British local authorities, etc. in connection with Government guaranteed euro-currency borrowing), we should have classified the loan as a balance-of-payments loan *pur et simple.* So a true project loan does not, in an *ex ante* sense, reduce balance-of-payments deficits of the countries sovereign to the borrowers: imports of such countries rise more or less 1:1 with the amounts of such loans. Admittedly, and irrelevantly, the position looks different *ex post*: the loan proceeds will be classified as capital inflow, offsetting 1:1 a part of the country's current-account deficit.

A correct interpretation of recycling, one in which the role of the banks becomes much diminished, would run like this. Treat that part of the oil-price generating exceptional O.P.E.C. balance-of-payments surpluses as a tax imposed upon importing nations. The notional O.P.E.C. taxing authority runs a budgetary surplus; that is why there is a recycling problem. For the most part, its surplus revenues take the form of cheques denominated in US dollars, the preferred O.P.E.C. currency. These become converted into interest-bearing euro-dollar accounts. At that point in the scenario, euro-banks will have excess liquidity. Their assets and liabilities will have expanded by the amount of the O.P.E.C. deposits. U.S banks will be unaffected in the aggregate. So an expansionary process will develop in money and securities markets until equilibrium liquidity-ratios are restored. The case simply is one of re-intermediation, so thoroughly studied in Chapter 2.

From a fiscal point of view, then, the O.P.E.C. scenario is, at least according to conventional keynesian reasoning, contractive; elementary textbooks explain the contractive consequences of an increase in taxes not nearly matched by increased public-spending. From a monetary point of view, the events are stimulatory; re-intermediation leads, *ceteris paribus*, to excess demand in securities markets. If one were rash, one might say that this analysis suggests why, since the big increase in the oil price, the world has experienced such slow growth and such high inflation.

Is O.P.E.C. a Cartel? Professor Stigler[4] and others have written excellent précis of the economics of cartels and price-leadership. Here we need only be concerned with implications of the correct analyses without repeating them. If O.P.E.C. best fits models of cartels, then O.P.E.C. probably will prove unstable and it well might be appropriate to the self-interest of such oil importers as the United States to exploit unstable features of the condominium. If O.P.E.C. best fits models of price-leadership—as I think it does—then the United States and others should assume that O.P.E.C. will prove stable as long as Saudi Arabia is stable. The implications for economic policy obviously are great.

Cartels result from concerted restrictive practices of producers who otherwise would comprise a workably competitive industry. Cartels characteristically are unstable for at least two reasons. Revenues from incremental sales will exceed incremental costs of production—if the sales are made *near* official prices. And, in the nature of a cartel, the cartel-price will be set as close as is feasible to the price charged by a notional monopolist; a monopolist would take account of effects of price cutting (necessary to expand sales) on revenues otherwise attainable; a monopolist's marginal revenue will be equated with his marginal cost so that his price will exceed his marginal cost; no amount of qualification and deepening of the analysis changes the thrust of this argument. Secondly, cartels characteristically are unable to prevent *entrance* into their industry. Up to the point where production quotas have shrivelled so much that the high price does no more than offset high overhead costs per unit (brought about, of course, by diminished quotas), there is a strong incentive, in the classical description, for outsiders to deal themselves into the game.

It will be evident to newspaper readers that it is not easy to deal one's self into the crude-oil production game. So the second source of cartel-instability can be put aside, at least in the medium run.

The first sort of instability cannot be evaluated until the global crude-oil industry is modelled. So it behoves us to probe more deeply into characteristic relationships between cartel members. The most important such characteristic is crucial here and indeed comprises a negative property: *lack of dominance by any member or small node of members. And* the obverse of this property lies at the heart of the preconditions for a price-leadership mode.

Domination can be exercised in at least two modes. One mode is *coercive*, the other *quasi-permissive*.

A few leading firms might be able to compel lesser firms to toe the line on prices and to restrict output simply by threatening otherwise to cut prices to the latter's clients, to saturate their markets through media blitzes, etc. The upshot might possess a certain stability; it certainly will be full of tension. The coercive mode is less feasible in most Western countries than in the past and indeed probably is out of the question for the most part in the United States and Britain for example. Nor does it seem pertinent to the crude-oil industry as it now stands.

Quasi-permissive price-leadership, a form of the second mode of domination, proves highly pertinent to 'oil'. Consider an industry in which a certain producer has, at least in the long run, the ability uniquely to produce at substantially lower unit cost than the others and, for practical purposes, without limit. It would be feasible for such a producer to announce that it would meet all demand at a certain price. No other producer would undercut that price: he can sell all he wants at the 'decreed' price. No other producer would quote higher: the Leader is prepared to meet *all* demand at the decreed price. The resulting system would be perfectly stable, lacking any element of tension.

Why should the Leader offer such seemingly generous terms to the other, inferior producers? True, if the Leader calculated that some price below minimum average cost of any other producer would maximize his profits, he would take all of the market for himself. For the exercise to be interesting, we must stipulate that the Leader's interest requires a price that other producers profitably can quote. Then the price-leadership scheme just outlined would offer the benefits of stability and predictability.

The quasi-permissive mode seems to fit the facts, in a longer run, of the crude-oil industry quite well. Saudi Arabia has immense proved reserves and is believed to have much larger unproved reserves, all readily and very cheaply extractable. Nor would it appear that it is in the interest of the ruling Saud family fully to exploit the purely financial potential of its superb oil position. The more rapidly Arabia develops, the more rapidly the numbers of bourgeois and technocrats grow, the more tenuous will become the country's political regime. Less sentential, the absorptive capacity of the Arabian economy, based on so small a population relative to its resources, will be limited even in a longish run. And, in any event, it would be easy for the regime to satisfy whatever are the material aspirations of its subjects, most of whom are deeply religious, at say an $8 a barrel price of oil. It is easy for Saudi Arabia to live with the *derived demand curve* of a price leader, *derived-demand* because the Leader characteristically subtracts the *supply of others* from total demand in calculating 'his' quantity demanded at a given price. It is hard to imagine a situation in which a government could more easily subordinate purely-economic considerations to political/strategic/ideological considerations. Nor should one ignore the natural fears of the Saudi regime of the consequences of radicalization of much of the Arab world, and other parts of the third world, that would follow from any marked decline in the price of oil: Saudi Arabia is militarily fragile; it might, in any case, find it hard to survive in a thoroughly hostile environment.

Willy-nilly, Saudi Arabia would appear to be a classical price leader. So it would appear that the O.P.E.C. structure is not a cartel and that O.P.E.C. is, from the point of view of economic analysis, highly stable. The implications for, say, American policy are quite obvious, but do not belong to the domain of this book.

9 Efficiency

9.1 Primary Remarks

The study of economic efficiency has illuminated all sorts of objective resource-allocation problems in industry, war, government, etc. Another pay-off has been growing understanding of the reasons why many real-world problems are not soluble at all. Thus consider a basic textbook-like problem in economics.

A firm's total revenue is some function, f(p), of the price it charges. Its total costs are a function of how much it produces, in turn determined by p. Costs $= F(p)$; profit $= f(p) - F(p)$. For profits to be maximized it is necessary that $f'(p) = F'(p) = 0$; the marginal profitability of any price change must be zero.

The problem can be solved as it has been put. But in the real world the firm will not *know* the properties of either function; it will not know whether there are functions (!). Much will depend on the amount of free information and the costs, relative to pay-offs, of getting more information. The firm's management will be able to do no more than grope towards one of the more favourable feasible outcomes.

The concept, *competitive equilibrium,* has massive spin-off. The principles of management of an enterprise large enough too have branches engages the competitive-equilibrium idea. It is impossible to understand such companies as IBM, Bank of America *et al.* without knowing something about competitive equilibria.

9.2 Development of the Efficiency Concept

Our development of the concept of efficiency in economics will lead to a good grasp of the characteristics of an admittedly idealized competitive industry. Then we shall move on to study of the properties of an economy that is competitively organized, working against benchmarks established by Vilfredo Pareto. These benchmarks will comprise a metric spanning a number of problems in economic policy, including taxes and subsidies, problems in private versus social costs, indelibly associated with Professor Pigou and Professor Frank Knight, and leading to some analysis of the relationship of property alignments and property law to efficient use of resources in a profit-maximizing environment, and finally (in this truncated conspectus) to some remarks on minimum-wage legislation, perhaps anticipated in Chapter 7.

Think of a firm that produces a number of products, using a number of variable inputs, together with some inputs fixed in supply. Perhaps there are two inputs, y_1 and y_2. Or we may be considering any pair of inputs, other input-utilization rates being given. Then Figure 9.1 applies.

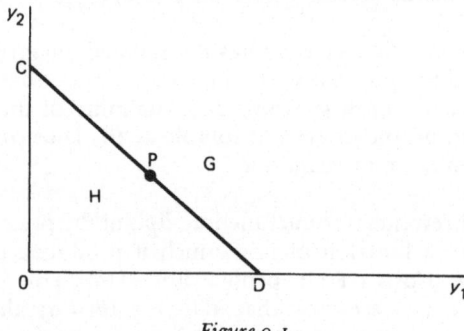

Figure 9.1

The sub-problem is to produce whatever is produced at minimum cost.

The lines parallel to CD in Figure 9.1 are iso-cost lines. All points belonging to CD lead to the same total expenditure on variable inputs Y. All points belonging to any line parallel to CD lead to the same total expenditure on variable inputs Y. The common slope of lines like CD is determined by the price to the firm of input y_1 relative to that of y_2.

Exercise. Draw a line like CD on the assumption that $p_1 = p_2$; then assume that $p_1 = 2p_2$.

Region G contains input combinations whose cost is at least as great as that attached to CD. Region H contains input combinations whose cost is no greater than that attached to CD. (CD is in H and G.) No point in H costs more than any point in G.

Technicians are able to ascertain that the point x* in the multidimensional set of productions X cannot cost less than the cost associated with CD, that the solution to the sub-problem is a point like P, that the solution lies in G.

Call this minimized cost v^*. Consider the set of input combinations capable of producing x^*; all these points will belong to G. Note their costs. Subtract $v^\bullet$ from each v thus obtained. The minimum on the set $(v - v^\bullet)_G$ is at P: $(v^\bullet - v^\bullet)_G = 0$. Now consider all the points belonging to H. Subtract the v values associated with these points from $v^\bullet$. All the differences $(v - v^\bullet)_H$ will be negative, except at P: $(v^\bullet - v^\bullet)_H = 0$. The maximum of the set $(v - v^\bullet)_H$ is at P.

The result is characteristic of a crucially important set of efficiency problems in economics. P is a *saddle point* in the counterpart problem that can be associated with efficiency problems in economics *if* production possibilities obey restrictions so that it is not possible to improve returns to effort as scale increases or as more of one input is used relative to another (going back to experiments of von Thünen). And, if certain other properties, permitting obedience to mathematical requirements like connectedness, continuity and so forth, requirements that are no more rigorously explored in many advanced texts than here, appertain, then problems of this sort can be completely solved—if the data-set is complete; it never is. Similarly for 'consumer' problems.

The complete, albeit simplified, problem for the firm is to maximize

$$R - C = \Pi \tag{9.1}$$

where R = revenue, C = cost and Π = profit.

The competitive firm will, at best, be able to achieve zero-profit, $\Pi = 0$ And the sense in which indeed a competitive firm in equilibrium earns zero profit is both rather special to economics and extremely important as a basis for correct decision making in industry and in policy-formation. A gloss is to be supplied at once.

Correct investment decisions—whether private or public—result from a continuous exercise like the following.

The firm, defined simply as a charged economic particle employing resources in order to maximize its net worth, would, in an ideally frictionless world, continuously contemplate its input/output array. Recognizing inevitable lags between taking and implementing decisions, the firm first asks whether resources now under its control are being optimally employed. Optimal resource-employment in the short run could, if one had all the data one never has, be ascertained by solving certain *programmes*. In the solution, resources are assigned *shadow prices*. Activities (an *activity* is a way of doing things and, obviously, involves using inputs to obtain outputs) that should be undertaken will show values, at the levels at which they should be operated, equal to the imputed worth of the resources they employ; in the solution the maximized 'shadow' pay-off is *zero*.

The firm's investment decisions flow naturally from the paradigm for resource deployment. Values to the company of incremental resources are compared with the resources' market values. The firm will surrender resources to the market so long as 'shadow' values are less than market prices; it will take resources off the market so long as shadow values exceed market prices. The calculations are 'at the margin' and so involve tiny steps: 'a little bit more or a little bit less'.

Strictly, the analysis should concern resource-*rents; services* of resources are being evaluated. But many resources are not hired out. So rents are *imputed* to owned, or to contemplatedly-owned, resources. The imputation is comprised of depreciation and interest costs: linkage finally has been established between financial and 'real' markets.

It is obvious that marginal profit from resource-acquisition should be zero: acquisition should continue so long as it is profitable. Less obviously, it always is possible to offer a zero-profit interpretation of a firms overall results. A hypothetical share-market illustration will develop the argument.

Companies A and B each employ resources costing $10 million. Company A earns $1 million annually; B earns $2 million. A fits exactly the zero-profit criterion for competitive equilibrium: the resources employed by A could earn $1 million p.a. in alternative uses; a rational A would impute zero-profit to its operations. B's case is farther from the surface. The share market will assign a $20 million valuation to B-capital, $10 million representing 'goodwill' or some other intangible asset. B shareholders may have paid $20 million for their shares. Anyhow book capital must be sharply distinguished from the premium over book'. Otherwise one might commit the solecism of 'discovering' that all companies have the same rate of return on capital (!). The $10 million B-premium is an *economic rent*; it is possible for a purely-competitive firm, owning some non-reproducible resource such as site-value, to earn economic rent (or counterpart, shorter-run, *quasi-rents*). The analysis of Section 9.2 strictly pertains only where all pertinent resources are reproducible.

So a purely-competitive industry cannot properly be defined in terms of zero-profit. It suffices to say that an industry is competitive if its members are price-takers and not price-quoters.

Returning to the mainstream of our analysis of economic efficiency and competition, one thinks of pay-offs to the entrepreneur (the firm) and to Nature relative to productions produced at minimum cost and sold at maximized revenue, here at market prices. The pay-off, z, to the entrepreneur belongs to the set Z. The other pay-off, y, to the set Y. For any outputs $\hat{x}, \hat{y} = -\hat{z}$ so that $\hat{y} + \hat{z} = 0$.

In the solution, ignoring the degenerate case, $x = 0$, $\bar{p} = (\bar{x}_1, \bar{x}_2, \ldots, \bar{x}_n); \ \bar{z} = \bar{y} = 0$. The maximum on the set Z and the minimum on the set Y is at $\bar{P}$. In the solution $\max(z) = \min(y)$.

The problem can be pulled together diagrammatically. In order to do so in two dimensions, the following specifications are necessary:

(1) For any set of outputs, *not* the optimal output(s), $\bar{x}$, then, for given

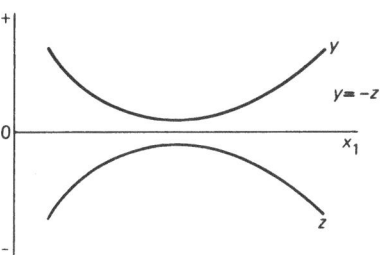

Figure 9.2

values for $x_2, x_3, \ldots, x_n, y > z$ for *all* values of x_1. See Figure 9.2. This is to say that costs exceed revenues at any point but $\bar{P}$; at $\bar{P}$, and only at $\bar{P}$, the value of the product is equal to the value of the resources used in producing it; everywhere else the resource-value exceeds the product-value. (Strictly, we should refer to *transferable* resources. Cf. *supra*.)

(2) For outputs $\bar{x}_2, \bar{x}_3, \ldots, \bar{x}_n$, where, of course, $\bar{x}_2, \bar{x}_3, \ldots, \bar{x}_n$ belong to $\bar{x} = \bar{P}$, $y > z$ for all x_1 *except* $\bar{x}_1$. For outputs $\bar{P} = \bar{x}$, $z = y$. See Figure 9.3.

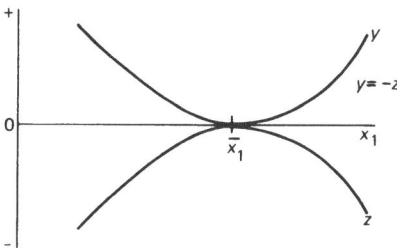

Figure 9.3

Before moving on to general or macro-efficiency (cf. Section 9.3), the micro-efficiency analysis, just completed, should be consolidated. This can be done rather attractively; highly topical illustrations will deepen the argument. The first illustration concerns the relationship, or lack of relationship, between *cash flow* and company investment in real resources. The second concerns the incidence of Reform in the real world; the second illustration flows into the analysis of Chapter 8; Fairness has evident relevance to it.

Cash Flow, etc.; The American Oil Industry, 1977–78

There are many arguments for free-market pricing of almost anything, including oil. The American oil industry stresses one of the few invalid arguments for removal of controls over the price of domestically-produced oil. It argues that its capacity to expand crude-oil production is keyed to its operational cash flow.

The factors promoting investment-profitability in an industry *are* likely also to increase cash flow. But the correct criterion for undertaking an investment is based on comparison of its discounted net proceeds with the expenditure necessary to generate them. A company may have a very substantial net cash flow, reflecting high rates of return on capital and equity. And that company, e.g., General Motors, may have a static business. Such a company usually pays out a large part of its profits in dividends. Another company may normally earn less on its capital, but it might have a growing business that eats up its cash flow and requires substantial annual capital-infusions for optimal exploitation of its opportunities. Such a company characteristically would repeatedly come to the market; its capital spending would not rationally be tied to its cash flow.

The economic solecism of the great oil companies is framed with a certain cunning: they know that the public does not grasp the difference between say *expense* and *amortization*; the public tends to equate items that drain cash. In so illiterate an economic climate, the oil companies reckon that a cash-flow/investment-expenditure script will play better than an increased profitability/investment-expenditure one. Demagoguery can create economic facts: the marginal efficiency of investment in exploration and the like will be pent up by politics; the capital markets indeed will be inefficient; funding will be inadequate.

Incidences and Burdens of Certain 'Reforms'

Recall that Company B earns an exceptionally high return on book equity and capital. One dollar spent on B shares buys only 50¢ of book value. And B shareholders bought their one million shares at 20.

Assume that B's high profitability results from protective-tariff cover and exemption from 'environmental' constraints.

After some reflection, the reader may retract hostility towards B—if he sees B as a set of shareholders and not as an organic entity. In modern economies, the most powerful companies are significantly owneed beneficially by holders typically much less wealthy than the owners of privately-held companies ('small businesses'); a giant B is likely to have many ordinary workers as beneficial owners; pension funds prefer publicly-held companies with large 'floats' (large masses of equity regularly traded in markets).

Probing into the last paragraph, nineteenth century bourgeois would have thought it absurd to put especial moral weight on effects on 'workers'. The bourgeoisie was concerned with *itself*. Western bourgeois today are very self-conscious, if not guilt-stricken, about their wealth, partly as a direct result of attacks by socialist intellectuals and partly because these attacks have put them on the tactical defence.

Continuing the core argument, present shareholders will have paid prices for their shares fully reflecting B's tariff protection and 'pollution' exemptions; they will be realizing only 'normal' returns on their B-investments. The beneficiaries of the discriminations benefiting B will long have been gone; the 'unfairly begotten' B-profits will have been capitalized by the market and taken off by earlier sellers of B stock; the discriminations underlie the premium over 'book' paid by present holders. They are at the mercy of 'reform'; reform threatens to impose upon them a $10 million capital loss (equal to the premium over 'book').

We have not proved that Reform should be eschewed. We merely have contemplated Reform in greater depth. Should there be Reform?

The discriminations favouring B lead to inefficient use of resources: resources are sucked into unnaturally-profitable B-activity; social and private costs are pried apart by the deviations from environmental controls benefiting B.

For many years, welfare economics has asked, 'should there be Reform?' And, being aware of the redistributive effects that punish the 'innocent' as well as the 'guilty', economists have focused on *compensation*. Compensation is as unlikely in the real world as it is intriguing to theorists. Indeed theorists have in fact centred on proto-compensation: criteria have been based on compensations that would be economically feasible regardless of politics. Thus reform of 'B abuses' would lead to an increment of national product whose present value exceeded $10 million: B shareholders *could* be compensated in full *and* the economy still would realize a surplus. What then *should* be done. I do not *know*. Do you?

Coda to Section 9.2

Perfectly-efficient share markets might force modification of the argument. Such markets would ingest the socio/political/economic nexus determining 'reform' probabilities and then discount B stock accordingly. Then B stockholders would have bought 'lottery tickets' with positive pay-offs under *status quo ante* and losses in case of thorough 'reform'.

9.3 Efficiency in the Sense of Pareto; Pareto Optimality

We have explored the idea that inefficiency, and perhaps only inefficiency, is intrinsically unfair. If resource-use is put into an efficient mode, time may resolve compensation conundrums; for many, the compensation *blocage* is unfair.

Pareto avoided 'compensation' by operating a *de novo* model: *nothing* is vested *de novo*. And 'good' men readily turn away from problems posed by Loathing and other unpleasantnesses and are prepared to confine analysis of Benevolence to footnote commentaries.

A Pareto optimum may be defined as a state in which it is impossible for one to attain a more-preferred consumption without at least one other person having to accept a consumption less-preferred by him. Pareto optima belong to the *possessive-individualist* ethos: the setting is egoistic; superegoistic feelings such as chagrin at the poverty of some and delight in that of others are ignored. Still the Pareto optimum idea is the supreme embodiment in economics of the ego principle.

The, very informal, discussion of efficiency in the sense of Pareto will move along these lines. A number of efficiency propositions will be stated. Each will be informally justified. Then each will be exemplified in the context of policy: efficient versus inefficient alternatives will be discussed.

For the last time (!), it must be stressed that there is no way to *prove* that the Efficient is the Good, that the efficient action is the right action, somehow teleologically mandated. Still it is easy to build an apologia for a discourse on efficiency:

> Any newspaper reader will see that governments, for example, rarely undertake inefficient programmes in the knowledge that these programmes indeed are inefficient. Minimum-wage legislation, for example is very inefficient; it does not seem to be perceived as such by most of the Congress or the electorate. Food subsidies are inefficient; only a few of those involved in the British political process appear to perceive subsidies correctly. Private-ownership economies are incorrectly believed to be inherently incapable of reconciling social and private cost; torrents of legislation, establishing huge new bureaucracies, have been generated in consequence.
>
> In other words, there is a large domain in the space of economic policy over which inefficient public actions are taken, not because of deliberate subordination to some higher (e.g. superegoistic) good but rather because of ignorance and confusion. It is obviously helpful to try to dispel these clouds.

9.4 Efficiency Propositions

9.4.1 Each Purchaser of Each Product should Pay the same Price

The performance of a competitive industry satisfies each efficiency condition so long as private and social cost are equal. Obviously, competition assures that all pay the same price for the same thing—noting that two physically-identical objects in different places at the same time are *not* the same things economically, just as physically-identical objects delivered to the same place at different times are not the same.

Say that C is charged x pence per loaf of bread whilst D is charged $x - y$ ($= z$) pence. This would be inefficient in at least two ways. (i) If the value of the resources used in a loaf of bread ('at the margin') is x pence, D would be consuming material worth z pence to him and x pence to the society; rearrangement would permit D and the society to achieve more-preferred consumptions. (ii) If C and D could make a market cheaply enough, they would trade off consumptions; D would supply C with bread and C would supply D with generalized purchasing power, i.e. money. If resources are efficiently allocated, actual markets exhaust the potential *gains from trade*.

What if C is rich and D poor?

It is better to be rich. Still, unless C simply is to be injured, the cost to him of a given real transfer to D ought to be minimized. Cost-efficiency requires that C and D pay the same prices for what they buy; cost-efficient compassion calls for lump-sum grants, not subsidies, to be offered to D.

By way of proof, assume that D now buys 200 loaves of bread per annum at 15p per loaf, that D spends £30 p.a. on bread. Next assume that a subsidy of 2p a loaf is offered to D. If D's bread-demand is perfectly inelastic, so that he continues to buy but 200 loaves, the upshot will be that of an annual cash-grant of £4. D will have a call on goods he values at more than their £4 social-worth.

In general D will buy more bread. D will value each additional loaf at less than 15p, the social cost of production. D gladly would accept a cash grant of less than the society's cost of providing his subsidy. Subsidies are inefficient.

A related fallacy dominates American discussion in 1977 of energy-pricing. It is widely agreed that efficiency requires a petrol price of at least $1 a gallon. *And* it is said that such a price would be unfair to the poor. No! Prices neither are fair nor unfair; they may be efficient or inefficient. If D is buying y gallons each year at $0.65 and would buy $y - v$ ($= u$) gallons at $1, he would value the $0.35 per gallon subsidy at rather less than its cost of (0.35)·(y)$ per annum. Why?

D values the 'last' gallon he uses at $0.65; the $0.35 subsidy on the yth gallon has *no* value to D.

If perceived social justice, here *distributive justice,* requires that the 'poor' be helped, this can be done efficiently through cash-grants. Welfare and Efficiency are complementary, not competitive, concepts.

9.4.2 Indirect Taxation is Inefficient

No real-world tax is *purely* direct. Thus income taxes are excises on work (or subsidies to leisure).

Anciently, excise (indirect) taxation was imposed in ways much lessening its inefficiency: the Crown, concerned to maximize its revenues, taxed (or monopolized) products such as salt and tobacco because their demand was inelastic; the Crown willy-nilly made indirect taxation as efficient as possible. Today, cigarettes and spirits are heavily taxed importantly because their consumption is deemed unhealthy or immoral. Indeed if such censorious motives were to become fulfilled, the taxes would yield nothing: there would be no consumption of cigarettes and spirits.

Can it be inefficient to deter citizens from contracting lung cancer? Persons, expecting to die *someday* and knowing that many pleasures (cf. private flying) shorten actuarial expectations of life, choose to smoke; this much is consistent with the practice of an efficiently liberal society. Still, 'superego' aside, there are 'efficiency' grounds for discouraging smoking, Russian roulette, etc: habits promoting lower life expectancy lead to the equivalent of emigration of skilled workers; premature emigration towards the Big Sky is like the Brain Drain.

It remains to offer a simple proof of the inefficiency of indirect taxation. Consider a bottle of whisky absorbing resources valued at £1.50. A tax of £5 is imposed. Persons paying £6.50 a bottle—and thus revealed to value it at at least that price—consume a product with a social cost of only £1.50. Say that a drinker consumes 50 bottles a year, thus paying £250 in taxes. Confront him with the option of paying a direct tax of £250 and confronting a whisky price of £1.50 after repeal of the excise. Will he accept the option? Yes. He will look forward to rearranging his consumption. The state's revenues will be unaffected.

9.4.3 *Prices should Equal Marginal Costs of Production*

(We abstract from unrealistic cases in which prices are unequal, but proportional, to marginal costs.)

Recall the cartel discussion of Chapter 8. Members of a competitive industry know that, collectively, they are producing more than would maximize industry-profit. This might even seem inefficient *to them*.

Reculer pour mieux sauter. Consider an industry so simple that total cost is measured by the formula, TC = (industry-output) × $3: if one million units are produced each year, total annual costs will be $3 million. (Private and social costs are assumed here to be the same.) The *opportunity cost* of production in the industry, at the margin, will be $3; the value of the services of resources required to produce a unit of product H, a valuation based upon the market's appraisal of the use-value of produce other than H that could be produced by these resources (always at the margin) will be $3. So long as the market is willing to pay at least $3 for another unit of H, more H should be produced: the market-value, the use-value of additional H then will exceed that of forgone produce. Nor should production be carried beyond the point where the *demand price* is at least $3. *And* a competitive industry will adhere precisely to these social efficiency conditions: profit-maximizing firms will expand production when price exceeds marginal cost and contract it when marginal cost exceeds price.

It becomes easy to see how competitors might perceive aggregate output to be inefficiently high; and why that perception is socially specious. Output restriction would increase industry profit and, indeed, output would fall in the wake of an excise tax, here a privately-imposed excise tax measured by the premium borne by price over its competitive norm. We have seen that all excise taxes are inefficient.

There always have been certain tensions between producer- and consumer interests, reflected in the common law of England's abhorrence of engrossing, later to be codified and expanded in the American antitrust law, in turn later imitated by British, continental, and European Community monopolies acts.

9.4.4 Wage Rates should be Equal to Open-Market Supply-Prices of Workers

Pressures for *minimum-wage legislation* usually come from trade unionists. The core of a canonical analysis of such legislation consists of *variegation* of labour. Consider bricklaying. Brown can lay x bricks during a working day; Green $2x$. Green would command a higher wage than Brown in an open market. There is no more *a* wage-rate for bricklaying than *a* price for cars. Each of us, *comme* labourer, is unique. And each of us, *comme* self-promoter, would be pleased if key rivals had to increase their supply-prices.

The natural rivals of mature, able-bodied workers, aside from other such workers, likely to be fellow trade unionists, are youngsters, pensioners, immigrants (often inept in their new tongue) *et al.* In the United States, for example, ample financial support for campaigns against 'sweated' labour can be obtained from Liberals; in June 1977 the American Secretary of Labour, Mr Marshall, proposed that *global* minimum wages be established. The inevitable consequence of success would be heightened unemployment amongst 'fringe' workers, or workers in less-developed economies, forced to demand uneconomic compensation.[1]

The analysis of minimum-wage legislation illuminates the South African *Apartheid* regime. True, white South African workers, although fearful of open competition with non-whites, do *not* demand that the latter be forced to quote infeasible supply-prices; racial attitudes preclude such demands. Instead, non-price rationing is used: thus, the Labour Reserve Laws and the like. Still minimum-wage legislation in Europe and America comprises an analytical counterpart to the South African *Apartheid* laws; they are linked by a common exclusionary principle. Science ignores distinctions between motor-forces of action that cannot be inferred directly from the actions themselves.

It cannot surprise the economic theorist that the South African business community has been a quite liberal force: few businessmen would prefer to pay higher wages to factory workers in order to get household servants more cheaply.

9.4.5 Tax Treatment of Various Activities should not Reflect Social Attitudes or 'Felt Needs'; cf. Depletion Allowances for Oil Producers

Completing our examples of possessive-individualist foundations of the efficient economy, we take up a variant of the excise-tax/subsidy problem. It seems natural under a political consensus that there is an energy crisis, that energy-source-creative activity should be encouraged.

For some years, oil exploration in the United States was heavily subsidized by depletion allowances greatly reducing tax liability. The allowance was inefficient:

> Under parity of tax treatment, Enterprises E and F each would invest $20 million all told and earn 20 per cent per annum ($4 million) on this capital before income tax, taken to be imposed at a flat rate of 50 per cent; rates of return after tax would be 10 per cent.
>
> Assume that F becomes tax-exempt and that the market discounts after-tax earnings at 10 per cent. F may find it optimal to go to the market for $15 million in additional capital, earning 15 per cent on average and 10 per cent at the margin, before *and* after taxes.
>
> E-capital will be more productive at the margin than F-capital; *efficiency* requires that they be equally productive at the margin. The tax discrimination will perpetuate an inefficient allocation of resources.
>
> (Analogously, it is inefficient to subsidize eleemosynary and other 'good' institutions.)

And oil-exploration activity was carried on at less productive margins than were fully-taxed ones.

The 'oil' problem has strategic ramifications. Many years ago Winston Churchill put the British Government into British Petroleum. The Teapot Dome scandals of the Harding Administration (1921–23) concerned U.S. Navy oil-reserve lands.

It seems incontestable that the state properly can—in the full context explored in Chapter 8; 'Beyond the Pleasure Principle'—overturn market verdicts on strategic materials. Even if a 1957 entrepreneur were perspicacious or premonitory enough to visualize the way in which the oil economy was turned upside-down after the Yom Kippur War of 1973, he would not have *acted* if he had thought all this highly unlikely. The state, The Guardian of Continuity is sworn to a different calculus.

So 'efficiency' properly can become pre-empted in a superego orientated society; but the pre-emptions may be unsound. The so-called energy crisis in the United States *circa* 1977 supplies a monumental example. American politics have clogged up exploitation of American energy sources for at least 20 years. Natural-gas prices have been screwed down, much discouraging exploitation; offshore oil operations have almost been paralysed; nuclear-power development is hopelessly short of earlier projections; American companies are aborting further investment in nuclear power. The American energy 'crisis' of 1977 would have been far less acute if a thoroughgoing free-market (possessive-individualist/egoistic) regime had prevailed throughout.

9.4 Social Cost and Private Cost

This section evokes the shade of Professor Pigou much as the last did that of Pareto:

> Paper mill P, situated well upstream on River R, is highly successful. P emits large quantities of noxious effluvia into the R. As a result, the R's downstream recreational value is much less, as are downstsream site-values, partly because the polluted state of the R substantially increases business costs of downstream enterprises, etc.

The cost of P-operations as they appear to P, their private cost, surely is less than their social cost. Indeed P's private cost may seem *inherently* less than its social cost. But it is not: the 'property latticing' must be analysed more deeply; one of the more interesting new directions in the theory of economic policy has emerged from intense scrutiny of this latticing.

Some Law and Economics

Quite recently, the scales have fallen from the eyes of many economists who long had analysed 'efficiency' independently of 'property latticing'. Thus,

> if the only economic elements were P and a downstream property, Z, what would happen if P and Z fell under common ownership?

Rational exploitation of the properties would require that full account be taken of effects external to P but internal for Z: the *external diseconomies* of P's operations would become *internalized;* 'external' is relative to property-latticing.

In science, only *stable* equilibria are interesting; only if displacement from an equilibrium state sets up a field of force impelling the system towards that state is 'equilibrium' interesting. Hence the query, 'if P and Z are not initially under common ownership will they move towards common ownership?' In a simplified model, 'yes'. But the generalization to complex real-world situations is not robust. The line of thought under scrutiny is fascinating but not compelling.

The property P + Z is worth more than P and Z taken apart. So, if the shares of P and Z are traded, one of two 'jointure' scenarios will ensue. The boards will agree to a merger: P profitably can offer more for a controlling interest in Z than the shares are worth to Z shareholders who will be glad to accept less than Z is worth to P. Or the shares of both companies will be acquired by buyers contemplating merger and hence willing to pay more for them than they now are worth.

Two observations consolidate the argument.

(1) The strong anti-merger bias of the American Government deters internalization of external diseconomies and so promotes inefficient use of resources.

(2) 'Internalization' *could* result from agreements between independent companies P and Z. P could have two revenue-sources: (i) sales of P products; (ii) collection of bribes from Z. Starting with mere maximization of isolated P-profits, P might calculate the loss to isolated profit and the gain to Z-profit from a small reduction in P's pollution-activity; this defines the maximum 'marginal' bribe that can be collected from Z. After a series of iterations, further reduction in pollution activity will charge isolated profit more than it will gain in bribes. The resulting equilibrium will be the same as the P + Z one.

The argument is bizarrely intriguing. But profound changes would have to occur in case law, statutes and *mores* for the 'bribe' modality to become important.

Final Remarks on Spontaneous Internalization of External Diseconomies: 'Fascinating but not Compelling'

We turn to real-world problems like traffic congestion, noise, smog, ugliness, rudeness, etc. Contemplate a frequent, and galling, sight: a pedestrian carrying a blaring transistor radio. It would be hard to set up efficient procedures for bribing him. And there is a strong moral consensus against such appeasement and for state intervention.

Consider next the problems typified by the *Concorde* controversy, centred in New York, over the supersonic plane's landing rights. This problem cannot feasibly be attacked through a vast set of individual compacts. Part of the explanation is based on another new direction in the theory of economic policy: there now is a large literature on the cost of information relative to its productivity, the ways in which densities and spans of markets become determined by transactions costs and the implications of the inevitable uncertainties and imperfections of information that gets assembled.

The algorithm of the fable would have British Airways and Air France negotiate with the millions of affected persons; the already dynamic American law industry would get a fresh fillip. Of course, the only remotely feasible modality would be based on *class actions*. But their inherent aggregativeness puts such actions into the domain of old-fashioned state intervention.

Recapitulating, one thinks of a vector measured by polar coordinates: its direction is defined by the angle θ; its length by r. Recent work on ways in which freely-operating markets could internalize seemingly inherent external diseconomies does establish a valuable new direction. But one must be sceptical about the distance economic policy can travel in that direction. The necessarily primitive channels of real-world politics soon would be clogged. Indeed there is an eerie unreality about the projections of this theory into policy-space. It won't play in Peoria ... or Coventry.

Notes

Chapter 2 The Logic of Money and Finance

1. The reader will want to work out a case in which C tries to expand its B̄-credit without contracting its B-credit. The resulting *re-intermediation* effects will be no greater than if C wanted to expand its B̄-credit at the expense of its B-credit.

Reserve-requirements tacitly are the same for all kinds of clearing-bank deposits in the text's analysis.

The text's results are invariant against a stipulation that B̄ must be paid in B̄ funds. B and B̄ funds would trade at par so long as they were thought equally capable of being reducible to legal tender; B-elements always could buy B̄ funds by tendering B-funds at par in the open market.

2. Laymen stress too much the daily closing prices of securities. Closing prices no more reflect the full set of supply/demand data available to an omniscient than do 11.15 prices. The last transaction's price may have been 27. The specialist, at the close, may have had buying orders for 20,000 units at 27 and selling orders for 30,000 units at 27 or more; buyers *bid* 27 and sellers *asked* 27 in Wall Street parlance. So the stock might be *quoted* '26¾ bid; 27 asked'. The quotation would reflect the market-maker's book: there is excess supply at 27. The market-maker does not want to risk taking in too much stock: he informs would-be sellers that they must accept a price of 26¾.

Keen observers might place more weight on the chance that the stock will open at less than 27 tomorrow; keen and prudent observers will keep in mind all the many things that could transpire overnight; naive observers will stress the 'last transaction' price, 27, neglecting the state of the market-maker's book.

3. Conventionally, the scenario implies a net capital gain of $125: gross gains of $625 were realized in sales at $98; members of the private sector had book losses of $500 when the 4,000 units they purchased at $98 fell back to $97.875.

Would a rational public treat its net worth as having increased just because central-bank credit increased by more than the market value of public debt held by the public decreased? Domestic central bank credit is not a productive resource. It cannot be converted into real assets. It does not enlarge the possibilities of production.

4. A trick of economic reasoning shows that fiscal policy *à outrance* will not become stalemated by effects of concomitant reductions in private spending. *Gross* investment expenditures can be no less than *nil*. Any 'crowding out' of this sort would exhaust itself once gross private capital expenditures fell to zero.

Chapter 3   Money Supply Control in the U.S.

1. Cf. M. L. Burstein, *Economic Theory: Equilibrium and Change* (London: John Wiley; 1968), ch. 13.

2. The text works out an instance in which the expected change is *nil*. This is done in order to minimize the necessarily substantial complexity of the exposition. The reader will be able to work out non-nil cases.

3. Strictly, arbitrage operations concern 'sure things'. The process described in the text is somewhat speculative. Similarly, in Wall Street, if X Company proposes to buy all the shares of Y Company by exchanging X shares for Y shares 1:1, and if X's offer is accepted by Y, and if 1·25 Y shares now are valued equally with 1 X share, then, if a trader sells short 100 X shares while buying 100 Y shares, he is called an arbitrageur. But the proposed merger might be blocked by the Government, perhaps on anti-trust grounds. The trader's position is risky to some degree.

4. Cf. James Meigs, *Free Reserves and the Money Supply* (Chicago: The University of Chicago Press; 1962).

5. The scenario skims over the relationship between discount-rate, open-market strategy and market yields. Obviously, a central bank determined to make credit easier would also cut its discount-rate.

6. Cf. J. M. Keynes, *A Tract on Monetary Reform* (London: Macmillan; 1923).

7. Cf. M. Friedman and A. J. Schwartz, *A Monetary History of the United States* (Princeton: The Princeton University Press; 1963).

8. Recent discussion in the United Kingdom (cf., for example the very interesting Greenwell bulletins or, for that matter, numerous articles in *The Times, The Financial Times, The Economist* and other newspapers) puts much stress on the ways in which movements of the monetary aggregates can become strongly influenced by loan-demand by bank customers. This vector of influence, its direction being undesirable relative to the classical theory of central-bank policy, may importantly be determined by the eccentric definition of reserve-eligible assets now in force in Britain. The British reserve base is significantly endogenously determined. Cf. Chapter 4.

9. Interesting historical and analytical descriptions are found in J. M. Keynes, *A Treatise on Money* (London: Macmillan; 1930) and M. Friedman and A. J. Schwartz, *A Monetary History of the United States* (Princeton : The Princeton University Press; 1963). I glossed these and other sources, adding some further comments, in M. L. Burstein, *Money* (Cambridge, Mass.: Schenkman Publishing Co. 1963).

10. So called 'econometric', and hence inevitably 'computerized', studies of effects of interest rates on money-demand often are invalidated by choices of monetary aggregates including non-interest-bearing items (currency and current accounts) *and* interest-bearing items (e.g. deposit accounts, i.e. time deposits).

11. It seems quite well supported by empirical work that distinctly broad-gauged aggregates, including selected liabilities of non-banking financial institutions, would, if properly measured, comprise the short-list for 'M,' in the text. This is not surprising: the broader measures are the better credit proxies for example. Nor is it surprising that the caveat, 'if properly measured', is so important. The broader measures are harder to measure accurately promptly. All

things considered, the real world equivalent to M tends to be broader than M-1 and narrower than M-6 which is importantly influenced by non-banking liabilities.

Chapter 4 Money Supply Control in the U.K.

1. Warren L. Smith and Raymond F. Mikesell, 'The Effectiveness of Monetary Policy: Recent British Experience', *Journal of Political Economy*, vol. 65, No. 1, February 1957, p. 25. A rather lonely criticism of this sort of approach was made by J. R. Sargent in a letter to *The Economist*, 19 May 1956.

2. Clear explanations of special deposits are found in the Bank of England's *Quarterly Bulletin*, Dec. 1960, p. 18, and in W. T. Newlyn, *Theory of Money* (London: Oxford University Press; 1962).

3. Cf. W. M. Dacey, 'The Floating Debt Problem', *Lloyds Bank Review*, April 1956, pp. 24–38; also Dacey's *British Banking Mechanism* (London: Hutchinson; 1951), ch. 10. I Discuss the matter in M. L. Burstein, *Money* (Cambridge, Mass.: Schenkman Publishing Co.; 1963), pp. 311–13.

4. Issue of eligible commercial and trade bills by the non-banking public is, of course, a choice to make such holdings more *negative*.

The 'New Cambridge' theory associating balance of payments deficits with the Public Sector Deficit is significantly dependent upon a similar 'rigidity'. Cf. the text of Chapter 4 *infra*.

5. Sometimes interest rates rise because liquidity-preference grows. This may have happened in the U.S. in 1974. Such a situation is hard to identify. To the extent that it can be identified, a case can be made for stepped-up monetary-growth, promoted by official intervention. Such identification can be made with fair certainty only *post hoc* unfortunately.

6. G. T. Pepper and G. E. Wood, '"Keynesian" and "Monetarist" Indicators of the U.K. Economy', ch. 15 of Allingham and Burstein (eds.), *Resource Allocation and Economic Policy* (London: Macmillan; 1976) on p. 183. Cf. also their note on p. 198.

7. Bank of England *Quarterly Review*, 1976 (IV).

Chapter 5 Euro-currencies and Extensions

1. It is common to term such a deposit a euro-dollar deposit even if it is received in the Cayman Islands or at Singapore (although the designation asian-dollar is used sometimes). We shall cling to such usage. Our interest is in foreign-dollar-deposit logic. The chapter's exposition will be facilitated by a uniform designation of such deposits, viz. *euro-currency*.

2. To the extent to which $\hat{B}_r$ receives a cheque drawn on $\hat{B}_u$, the $\hat{B}$ disequilibrium-position will be unaffected.

3. J. G. Gurley and E. S. Shaw, *Money in a Theory of Finance* (Washington: The Brookings Institution; 1960).

4. Cf. Luigi Einaudi, 'The Theory of Imaginary Money', *Enterprise and Secular Change* (Homewood, Illinois: Richard D. Irwin, Inc.; 1952), pp. 229–61.

NOTES   161

5. Recent dirty-floating episodes have found 'American company' replaced by
'Electricité de France' (EDF), various British local authorities, etc. The process of
converting the loan-proceeds into French francs or British pounds creates demand for FF or sterling and counterpart supply of U.S. dollars, thus supporting
spot FFs or sterling.
6. Cf. Norway, Holland and Denmark. Britain, of course, is a perfect example of
a medium-sized, highly-open economy.
7. Cf. an interesting article by Samuel Brittan in *The Financial Times* dated 7 April
1977.
8. Cf. F. A. Hayek, Denationalisation of Money (London: The Institute of
Economic Affairs; October 1976).
9. In the United States the Hayekian Ideal can be at least partially attained
through trading in foreign-currency futures on the Chicago Mercantile
Exchange. If a dollar-lender wanted to assure himself of terms based on the
presumptively consensual projection of German inflation, he could contract to
deliver the proceeds of his dollar loan for marks at the maturity-date.
  Trading on the Chicago market during 1977 was blamed by the Canadian
Government for deterioration in the U.S. dollar value of the Canadian dollar.
The Diocletian theory of inflation always will be the most popular with
governments: governments always will blame even the measurements of inflation on faults amongst those governed; governments always will assume roles as
'inflation fighters' on the side of the forces of Light in Manichean struggles.
Most governments will inflate most of the time.

Chapter 6 Share Prices

1. Cf. M. L. Burstein, 'Monetary Policy, the Stock Market and the Real
Economy: A Keynesian Conspectus', in Michael Allingham and M. L. Burstein
(eds.), *Resource Allocation and Economic Policy* (London: Macmillan; 1976), pp.
153–63.
2. Franco Modigliani and Merton Miller, 'The Cost of Capital, Corporation
Finance and Theory of Investment', *American Economic Review* (48), June 1958,
pp. 261–97.
  A good starting point in this field is Myron J. Gordon, *The Investment, Financing and Valuation of the Corporation* (Homewood, Ill.: Richard D. Irwin, Inc.;
1962). Gordon's book, a bit dated now, is notably direct and succinct.
3. The public policy towards public debt also is illuminated by this analysis. If
citizens imputed public debt to themselves, public-debt holdings could not
properly be deemed part of individual wealth except to the extent that one held
more than one's share, implying that others held less than theirs. Nor would the
term-structure of public debt be important: citizens would make their own
micro term-structures.
4. Compare two companies each employing total capital of $1 million. The un-
geared company earns $120,000 p.a. Say that the geared company has borrowed
$900,000 of its capital at 10 per cent. If it earned $103,000 p.a. before interest
charges (hence 10·3 per cent on capital), it would show annual earnings of
$13,000 p.a. after paying interest (hence it would be earning 13 per cent on
equity). If profits before interest charges were to fall by $15,000 in both cases,
the ungeared company's profit would, of course, be $105,000—still respectable.

The geared company would *lose* $2,000; its profit would fall by more than 115 per cent. 'All they that take the sword shall perish with the sword.'

Chapter 8 Fairness

1. Cf. M. L. Burstein, *Economic Theory: Equilibrium and Change* (London: John Wiley & Sons; 1968), chs. 1 and 10.
2. Thus canon law, or the equity branch of civil law, are not sorts of nonsenses. The Bishop of Rome infallibly lays down laws that are consonant with the divine will if not divinely inspired. The equity courts have arrved at a set of decision rules based on what various chancellors felt truly was just. Generations of Jesuits and chancery lawyers have shown that bodies of law as positive as the proper law of the American Constitution can be generated by a process based on divinely-inspired tenets. Indeed the Mormon Church holds that the framers of the American Constitution proper (after all, some of the amendments are truly fatuous) were divinely inspired *au détail*. Since it is possible for anyone to *say* that anything is Just (I have wrestled with an angel of the Lord; the angel told me what is Just). The concept, Justice, seems irrelevant to legal science.
3. Cf. Michael Jefferson's contribution to Allingham and Burstein (eds.), *Resource Allocation and Economic Policy* (London: Macmillan; 1976).
4. Cf. George J. Stigler, *The Theory of Price* (New York: Macmillan; 1966).

Chapter 9 Efficiency

1. The Guaranteed Annual Income concept, strongly supported by Professor Friedman for example, reflects superegoistic concern about the slim pickings many low-skilled workers may have in free markets. And the concept is consistent with Efficiency: instead of imposing excise taxes on supply-prices of disadvantaged workers, lump-sum disbursements are made.

Glossary

Accelerator, the   The relationship between, say, expenditure on durable goods or capital-accumulation and the *change* in the desired stock position or in industrial output.

Activity, an   A precise, mathematically expressed, description of a way of doing things.

Autarchy   Economic autarchy implies that a national authority has absolute sovereignty so that it can make policy unilaterally. It never can.

Autocorrelation   A series is autocorrelated when previous values imply subsequent values.

Autonomous   An autonomous economic force operates on the system but is not affected by the system.

Banking School, the   A group of British writers, *circa* the 1840s and 1850s, critical of the separation of the departments of the Bank affected by the 1844 Act. They supported a *principle of reflux* favouring responsiveness of bank credit to demand. The principle is pernicious.

Bayesian theory   A Bayesian decision rule revises the initial probability-set in the light of sampling experience. This is contrary to classical statistical methods.

Capital–output ratio   The proportion borne by an underlying stock to a flow. If $1 million in capital is required to produce $100,000 in product annually, the ratio is 10.

Cash flow   Best thought of as profit plus depreciation and other notional items not requiring cash outlay.

Cash ratio   The proportion borne by a British bank's vault cash and balance at the Bank of England to its deposit liability.

Certificates of deposit   Negotiable interest-bearing deposits for term in relatively large denominations.

Competitive equilibrium   A price, or set of prices, equilibrating demand and supply when both sides of the market operate at all times relative to a quoted market price. Competitive traders take, but do not quote, prices.

Corset, the   A recently devised Bank of England practice requiring incremental *special deposits* from banks expanding 'too rapidly'.

Cost of capital   The charge, expressed as a per annum percentage rate, imposed by the Market upon a company's earnings in exchange for incremental capital. Cost of capital is most usefully perceived as a discount rate implicit in Market valuations. *But* future streams cannot be *known*; cost of capital is not explicit.

Covariance   The relationship between the movements of two or more variables. Covariance is *nil* when these movements are uncorrelated.

Covered positions   Hedged positions: if an American is owed sterling for 90-day delivery, he can *cover* his position by selling forward that amount of sterling for delivery against dollars in 90 days.

Crowding out   The extent to which increased public-sector borrowing-requirements may lead to reduced private-sector capital-formation.

Currency School, the   A group of British writers, *circa* the 1840s and 1850s, whose thinking became embodied in the 1844 Act. The currency principle called for monetary fluctuation to imitate the notional performance of a metallic currency. The Currency School played down bank deposits.

Current accounts   Called *demand deposits* in the United States.

Current account, the   That part of the balance of payments concerned with goods and services as against capital transfers.

Decision theory   A fairly recent body of formal analysis concerned with optimizing choice in the face of uncertainty and relative to imperfect, scarce information. Its major components are economics, statistics and mathematics.

Demand deposits   Called *current account* in the United Kingdom.

Deposit accounts   Called *time deposits* in the United States.

Disaggregation   The breaking down of such conglomerated concepts as gross domestic product into its components. Economics is notable for its massive, intractable *aggregation problems*.

Domestic credit expansion (DCE)   An artificial money-supply-like measure that adjusts money supply proper in phase with the current-account deficit of the Balance of Payments. It is favoured by the IMF and nobody else.

Duality (duals, dualism, etc.)   Many keyproblems in economic theory can be restated so that their *dual problems* have solutions equal in value to these *primals*. This line of analysis culminates the study of convexity properties in the application of mathematical analysis to economics.

Earnings (quality of)   Companies account for their earnings with differing conservatism. Earnings-quality is a rather euphemistic way of noting this.

Efficient markets   Prices determined in efficient markets fluctuate as new information is received, as unanticipatable corrections are made, in ways properly predicted or because of *random* shocks but *not* because of correction of avoidable errors. Efficient markets do not make avoidable errors; accordingly they cannot be 'beaten'.

Ego principle, the   A concept, rooted in the psychoanalytical literature, referring to promotion of one's perceived interests as these flow from self-consciousness and especially consciousness of self *vis-à-vis* others.

Endogenous   Endogenous variables become determined by the working out of an economic system.

Euro-currencies   Monetary claims generated by deposit of claims against banks of one country, and denominated in that country's money of account, with financial institutions in another country, the denomination of the resulting new claim is that of the deposited claim.

Euro-dollars   The most important of the euro-currencies.

Ex ante/ex post   A scheme of analysis first advanced in Sweden and discriminating sharply between planned (*ex ante*) and realized (*ex post*) outcomes.

Exogenous   An exogenous variable operates *autonomously* on an economic system.

External diseconomies Adverse effects on others' possibilities of transforming inputs into outputs caused by one's operations. (Cf. the 'paper mill' illustration of Chapter 9.)

External diseconomies, internalization of Revision of the ownership framework (lattice) so that a diseconomy becomes relevant to the optimizing calculus of the new entity. Cf. *merger* as per Chapter 9.

Federal funds Negotiable claims against the Federal Reserve System.

Federal funds rate The rate of interest charged for loans of Federal Funds.

Feedback The process through which measurable 'events' generated by the working of a system get fed back into it: public opinion affects politicians whose responses affect public opinion; etc.

Financement The process of financing.

Financial disintermediation or re-intermediation Transfers of claims against non-banks to banks (disintermediation) or of claims against banks to non-banks (re-intermediation).

Fundamental analysis (of stocks) Valuation of say shares based on application of economic theory and leading to portfolio selection based on the assumption that the market is inefficient.

Funding (of debt) Lengthening the maturity of outstanding debt.

Fungible (fungibility) In law, referring to the ability of one object to replace another (cf. one unit of currency versus another; *any* dollar will do). In finance, referring to ease with which an asset can be converted into money.

Game theory The theory showing optimal technique for forming strategies in highly abstract formalizations of such games as poker and having astonishing relevance for a vast range of problems. Now 'game theory' studies 'games' remote from those of ordinary experience.

Gearing (leverage) Gearing is measured by the ratio of borrowed to total capital. It gives *leverage*.

General-equilibrium theory The study of the formal properties of sets of prices and outputs equilibrating n markets simultaneously. Practical work in economics usually is based on the theory of isolated markets; this theory studies each market on the assumption that other prices and outputs are given.

Goodwill The difference between net worth and tangible net worth.

Holism Holistic interpretations of social 'organisms' treat these as having properties of their own, apart from the properties of their members.

Id, the The instinctive impulses of the individual.

Inflation-expectations This definition is obvious. What is important is that these expectations are formed individually; there is no proper sense in which a Market has *an* expectation (cf. *holism*).

Leverage The American locution is *leverage;* the British, *gearing*.

Liquidity preference A term used by J. M. Keynes to suggest the degree of preference, all else the same, for monetary over non-monetary assets.

Liquidity ratio, the The proportion borne by eligible assets of British clearing banks to their deposit liability.

Liquidity trap, the An expression not used by Keynes but which became common in keynesian economics and which refers to the possibility that liquidity preference will prevent the rate of interest on long debt from falling as low as would be needed for full employment.

Macro-economics The branch of economics concerned with the behaviour of aggregated statistics measuring the performance of the economy as against its members.

Marginal efficiency of capital '... I define the marginal efficiency of capital as being equal to that rate of discount which would make the present value of the series of annuities given by the returns expected from the capital-asset during its life just equal to its supply price'; J. M. Keynes, *General Theory*, p. 135.

Matrix of claims The array of cross-claims displaying credit taken and given between as many categories of economic actors as are wanted.

Micro-economics The branch of economics concerned with the behaviour of individual markets as determined by the principles of economic optimization as practised by individual economic particles.

Minimum lending rate (MLR) The rate of interest charged by the Bank of England to preferred borrowers and replacing Bank Rate.

Moments (e.g. of probability distributions) Measures of dispersion. The second moment is called the *variance* and is especially widely used in economic and financial analysis. The concept is especially important in portfolio selection: there can be trade-offs between expected returns and their variability.

Monetarism An unfortunate, but widely used, description of the views of Professor Milton Friedman *et al.* Monetarists put stress on money supply and are opposed to using interest rates as targets for monetary-policy strategies.

Monetary base What Professor Friedman calls *high-powered money*: for the most part, central-bank credit plus currency; that portion of the base controlled by banks becomes the American equivalent of the former British cash-base.

Multiple A share's price/earnings ratio is, in Wall Street, called its *multiple*.

Multiplier, the Some British observers call a share's p/e ratio its multiplier. By far the most important usage however, is that of keynesian theory: the investment multiplier indicates how much GDP will change as a result of a change in autonomous spending.

Objective function A mathematical formulation defining *pay-off* as a function of *outcomes*. A problem's solution obtains the largest *feasible* pay-off.

Open-market operation Securities transactions conducted by central banks in general money markets.

Ontological Concerned with essence of things or being in the abstract.

Opportunity cost The measure of an activity's cost cast up in terms of the value of opportunities forgone in order to operate the activity at its stated level.

Paradigm A pattern. Paradigms in economics concern exemplary schemes, suggesting whole classes of workings out.

Parameter (parametric) A quantity constant in considered instances, but varying in different cases. Parametric variables often are *controls* and should be sharply distinguished from *constants* of nature for example.

Propensity (to consume, invest, save, etc.) A locution of J. M. Keynes: '... the propensity to consume [is] the functional relationship ... between ... a given level of income ... and ... the expenditure on consumption out of that level of income', *General Theory*, p. 90.

Propensity to consume (etc.), Marginal The rate at which consumption changes with income, evaluated at some level of income and, in general, variant with income. The average/marginal distinction is *crucial* in economics.

Public sector borrowing requirement The text (especially Chapter 4) sometimes shortens this to 'public sector deficit'. The concept is obvious. It is important to distinguish that part of the PSBR resulting from transfer payments from that part resulting from expenditures on goods and services, just as it is important to distinguish revenues from taxes from those from sales of public-sector industries.

Quasi-rent   A rent resulting from a resource's temporary inelasticity of supply.

Randomization (e.g. of strategy)   Reversion to selection of sequences of actions at random. In this way one's moves can become unpredictable by the enemy, at the cost of being so by one's self.

Random walk   An example of a series of movements the 'values' of which could have been determined by a random roulette wheel so that 'future' cannot be predicted from 'past'.

Rational expectations   Sets of predictions by economic actors that represent the best use of existing data that could be made through intelligent use of the best existing theory.

Real estate investment trusts (R.E.I.T.s; pronounced 'reets')   American companies specialized to real-estate investment, conditional upon paying out almost all their earnings as dividends. The condition proved otiose in most instances: the companies had no earnings by 1975.

Rent (i.e. economic rent)   That part of the price paid for a resource in excess of its opportunity cost.

Residuals   Differences between actual results and those predicted by the model being operated.

Saddle point   'When the guaranteed minimum and maximum payoffs of Blue and Red are exactly equal, ... the game is said to have a *saddle point*, J. D. Williams, *The Compleat Strategyst*, p. 27. The saddle-point notion is embedded in duality.

Second best   A second-best optimum is one achieved relative to circumstances preventing attainment of the 'true' optimum: a cricket captain might be told to pursue his optimum strategy, given that his best fast bowler is going to be away in Australia on a promotional tour.

Shadow prices   A resource-valuation imputed by an 'internal' programme and often interpretable as a Lagrangian multiplier. A *shadow* price because this price is not arrived at in a market.

Sigma (σ)   Symbol for the standard deviation of a probability distribution so that variance is denoted σ^2.

Social cost (versus private cost)   Cost as perceived societally instead of from a purely individual viewpoint. Cf. *external diseconomy*; then social cost exceeds private cost.

Special deposits   Claims against the Bank of England held by clearing banks and which do *not* count against liquidity ratios, etc. These deposits are sterilized.

Specialist   A Wall Street locution referring to firms entrusted with making markets for shares. Specialists deal on their own account, taking in stock in order to prevent disorderly price declines and feeding out stock in the converse case.

Stability   A property of an economic model. A stable system will re-attain its solution-point if displaced from it—thus a stable equilibrium. There are many sorts of stability.

Stare decisis   Describing the determining role of precedent in the common law of England and then in America. *Stare decisis* once was important in the law of the American Constitution.

Steady state   A constellation of values, describing the state of a system, that endlessly repeats itself. Regular, unaccelerated motion is analytically like a steady state for most purposes.

Stochastic   Stochastic processes are influenced by random disturbances. They concern stochastic variables. An example of a stochastic process in economics would be the path traced out by capital expenditures. This path is influenced by forces taken to be random as well as by *systematic* actions.

Superego   'The super-ego is the highest mental evolution attainable by man, and consists of a precipitate of all prohibitions and inhibitions, all the rules of conduct which are impressed on the child by his parents and by parental substitutes. The feeling of *conscience* depends altogether on the development of the super-ego', A. A. Brill, 'Introduction' to *The Basic Writings of Sigmund Freud* (New York: The Modern Library; 1938), pp. 12–13.

Suppressed inflation   A state of persistent excess demand for goods and services not allowed to express itself through rising prices outside of black markets. Suppressed inflation expresses itself through queues, shortages, quality deterioration, delivery-delay, etc.

Symbiosis   Union between organisms each of which depends on the other. One might say that they feed off each other.

Synergism   *Not* the accepted notion, i.e. the doctrine that the human will cooperates with the divine spirit in the work of regeneration. *Rather*—in common 'scientific' usage—along the lines of serendipity: the way in which effort along one direction more or less accidentally enhances efforts along different directions.

Technical analysis (of stock trends)   Study of criteria for price-trend reversals based on the assumption that price-movements are altogether auto-correlated.

Teleological   Concerned with (the doctrine) of final causes and purposes.

Time deposits   The American locution for British *deposit accounts*.

Transfer payments   Payments, usually by governments, *not* for goods and services purchased, e.g. income-supplements or parental allowances. Not to be confused with the *transfer problem*. The latter is concerned with making feasible reparations payments, for example, from one nation to another: the constraint for the transfer problem is financial, not technical: e.g. where was the specie to be found to finance German reparations after the 1914–18 war?

Treasury View   The predominant view of the British Treasury *circa* 1920–30 that increased public spending would *crowd out* private spending 1:1. Cf. the *Macmillan Report*.

Variance   The square of the *standard deviation* of a statistical distribution. The standard deviation is obtained by extracting the root mean square of the deviations from the mean. It always is positive.

Velocity of monetary circulation   It is most unwise to try to interpret monetary velocity in 'physical' terms, as a turnover statistic for example. Rather it simply is the value for V that equates MV with PY in the canonical 'equation of monetary exchange'. There has developed a perversity in pseudo-monetary theory to the effect that central banks should alter their money-growth policies in response to shifts in measured velocity. In fact the only *raison d'être* for money-growth orientated policy is based on the relative accuracy of velocity-prognostication.

Zero sum   In a zero-sum game, the payoffs to the players aggregate to zero:

think of bridge. In matrices describing financial asset and liability holdings, grand totals are zero to the extent that the financial assets are comprised of obligations to pay and hence of liabilities within the system. There is much doubt about the proper way to treat treasury currency: is this a *net* asset?

Bibliography

Note to the Bibliography

The bibliography stresses books supplying applied-mathematical technique, together with some sources of simple and correct price theory and a smattering of other references.

The readers of a book like this typically have plenty of information; the press contains more than the facts. The readers do not want a *Dogmengeschichte*; they do want to sort out the mass of material in which they are awash. But the readers are variously prepared: some have good analytical, including mathematical, backgrounds; others are adept in informal economics; still others are informed and acute but technically unprepared. The bibliography provides 'tracks' for each of the three groups. And, tacitly, it disclaims any possibility that one can become learned in economic policy in the way that one might know the etymologies of numerous words. Instead it reflects the author's conviction that correct thinking about economic policy essentially is informed common sense *shaped* by techniques of analysis not at all peculiar to economics.

Mozart once wrote, 'if only all the world knew harmony!' A writer of a book like this will wish that readers typically had a lot of maths and liked maths. But typically they do not. The bibliography reflects my acceptance of this fact of life, together with my encouragement of its exceptions.

MB

Contents of the Bibliography

R. G. D. Allen, *Mathematical Analysis for Economists* (London: Macmillan; 1938).
R. G. D. Allen, *Mathematical Economics* (London: Macmillan; 1956).
W. J. Baumol, *Business Behaviour, Value and Growth* (New York: Macmillan; 1959).
W. J. Baumol, *Economic Dynamics* (New York: Macmillan; 1951).
W. J. Baumol, *Economic Theory and Operations Analysis* (Englewood Cliffs, N. J.: Prentice-Hall; 1961).

W. J. Baumol, *The Stock Market and Economic Efficiency* (New York: Fordham University Press; 1965).

Arnold Bernhard, *The Evaluation of Common Stocks* (New York: Simon & Schuster; 1959).

M. L. Burstein, *Money* (Cambridge, Mass.: Schenkman Publishing Co.; 1963).

M. L. Burstein, *Economic Theory* (London: John Wiley & Sons; 1968).

M. L. Burstein, contributions in Michael Allingham and M. L. Burstein (eds.), *Resource Allocation and Economic Policy* (London: Macmillan; 1976).

R. H. Coase, 'The problem of social cost', 3 *Journal of Law and Economics* 1 (1960).

Competition and Credit Control (Bank of England, 1975).

Paul H. Cootner (ed.), *The Random Character of Stock Market Prices* (Cambridge, Mass.: The M.I.T. Press; 1964).

W. M. Dacey, *The British Banking Mechanism* (London: Hutchinson, 1951).

W. M. Dacey, 'The floating debt problem', *Lloyds Bank Review*, April, 1956.

A. C. L. Day, *Outline of Monetary Economics* (Oxford: The Clarendon Press; 1957).

R. Dorfman, P. A. Samuelson, and R. M. Solow, *Linear Programming and Economic Analysis* (New York: McGraw-Hill; 1958).

R. D. Edwards and John Magee, *Technical Analysis of Stock Trends* (Springfield, Mass.: John Magee; 1966), 5th ed.

Luigi Einaudi, 'The theory of imaginary money', in *Enterprise and Secular Change* (Homewood, Ill.: Richard D. Irwin; 1952).

Irving Fisher, *Purchasing Power of Money* (New York: Macmillan; 1926).

Irving Fisher, *The Theory of Interest* (New York: Kelley and Millman, 1954).

Freud, Sigmund, *The Ego and the Id* (London: The Hogarth Press; 1950).

Freud, Sigmund, *Beyond the Pleasure Principle* (London: The Hogarth Press; 1950).

Freud, Sigmund, *The Future of an Illusion* (London: The Hogarth Press; 1949).

Freud, Sigmund, *The Basic Works of Sigmund Freud,* (translated and edited by A. A. Brill, New York: The Modern Library; 1938).

Milton Friedman and Anna J. Schwartz, *A Monetary History of the United States* (Princeton, N. J.: Princeton University Press (for the NBER); 1963).

Milton Friedman, *Lectures in Price Theory* (Chicago: Aldine Press; 1966).

Benjamin Graham and David L. Dodd *et al., Security Analysis* (New York: McGraw-Hill; 1962).

Myron J. Gordon, *The Investment, Financing and Valuation of the Corporation* (Homewood, Ill.: Richard D. Irwin; 1962).

John G. Gurley and Edward S. Shaw, *Money in a Theory of Finance* (Washington: The Brookings Institution; 1960).

G, Hadley, *Nonlinear and Dynamic Programming* (Reading, Mass.: Addison-Wesley; 1964).

Sir Roy Harrod, *Towards a Dynamic Economics* (London: Macmillan; 1948).

F. A. Hayek, *Denationalisation of Money* (London: The Institute of Economic Affairs; 1976).

J. Kemeny and J. Snell, *Mathematical Models in the Social Sciences* (Boston: Ginn; 1962).

J. M. Keynes, *A Tract on Monetary Reform* (London: Macmillan; 1923).

J. M. Keynes, *A Treatise on Money* (2 vols.) (London: Macmillan; 1930).

J. M. Keynes, *The General Theory of Employment, Interest and Money* (London: Macmillan; 1936; New York: Harcourt, Brace; 1936).

F. H. Knight, *The Ethics of Competition* (New York; Harper; 1935).

F. H. Knight, *Freedom and Reform* (New York Kennikat; 1947).

C. B. Macpherson, *The Political Theory of Possessive Individualism: Hobbes to Locke* (Oxford: The Clarendon Press; 1962).

Alfred Marshall, *Principles of Economics* (London: Macmillan; 1920), 8th edn.

James Meigs, *Free Reserves and the Money Supply* (Chicago: The University of Chicago Press; 1962).

Franco Modigliani and Merton Miller, 'The cost of capital, corporation finance and theory of investment', 48 *American Economic Review* 261, (June 1958).

W. T. Newlyn, *Theory of Money* (London: Oxford University Press; 1962).

G. T. Pepper and G. E. Wood, '"Keynesian" and "Monetarist" indicators of the U.K. economy', ch. 15 of Allingham and Burstein (eds.), *Resource Allocation and Economic Policy* (London: Macmillan; 1976).

A. C. Pigou, *The Economics of Welfare* (London: Macmillan; 1960).

Karl Popper, *The Poverty of Historicism* (London: Routledge and Kegan Paul; 1957).

'Radcliffe Report': Committee on the Working of the Monetary System, *Report* (London: Her Majesty's Stationery Office; 1959).

D. H. Robertson, *Money* (London: Pitman; 1948).

D. H. Robertson, *Banking Policy and the Price Level* (London: Staples Press; 1949).

Joan Robinson, *The Accumulation of Capital* (London: Macmillan; 1956).

Joan Robinson, *Essays in Marxian Economics* (London: Macmillan; 1949).

Joan Robinson, *Essays in the Theory of Economic Growth* (London: Macmillan; 1962).

Bertrand Russell, *A History of Western Philosophy* (New York: Simon and Schuster; 1945).

Jean-Paul Sartre, *Being and Nothingness* (New York: Philosophical Library; 1956).

R. S. Sayers, *Modern Banking* (Oxford: The Clarendon Press; 1951).

R. S. Sayers, *Central Banking after Bagehot* (Oxford: The Clarendon Press; 1957).

Robert Schlaifer, *Probability and Statistics for Business Decisions* (New York: McGraw-Hill; 1959).

Robert Schlaifer, *Introduction to Statistics for Business Decisions* (New York: McGraw-Hill; 1961).

George J. Stigler, *Theory of Price* (3rd edn. New York: Macmillan; 1966).

James Tobin, 'Inflation, interest rates and stock values', *Morgan Guaranty Trust Survey* (July 1974).

Jacob Viner, *Studies in the Theory of International Trade* (New York: Harper and Bros.; 1937).

W. A. Wallis and H. V. Roberts, *Statistics: A New Approach* (Glencoe, Ill.: The Free Press; 1956).

A. A. Walters, *An Introduction to Econometrics* (London: Macmillan; 1968).

Knut Wicksell, *Lectures on Political Economy* (Vol. 2) (London: George Routledge & Sons; 1935).

Knut Wicksell, *Selected Papers on Political Economy* (London: George Allen & Unwin; 1958).

J. D. Williams, *The Compleat Strategyst* (New York: McGraw-Hill; 1952).

Index of Subjects

Index of Names